Diane Franklin
London, November, 1976

Marxism
and
"Primitive"
Societies

Marxism and "Primitive" Societies

two studies by
Emmanuel Terray

translated by Mary Klopper

New York and London

Contents

Publisher's Introduction to the French Edition

The two studies presented here, "Morgan and Contemporary Anthropology" and "Historical Materialism and Segmentary and Lineage-Based Societies," were prepared at different times. They are independent of each other and can be read separately. Something should, however, be said to explain the association between them.

There is an objective explanation for this association, what could be described as an identical crisis of theory dominating both ethnology and anthropology, whether the researchers concerned are aware of it or not. It can be reduced to a question which can be simply formulated but which is very complex in its consequences and the tasks it imposes: In the study of "primitive societies" how relevant is historical materialism, the science of social development set out by Marx?

To be sure, the question has long been debated: it is known that non-Marxists reject the very possibility of posing such a question, while Marxists accept it and give an affirmative answer on principle. What is new in the present theoretical crisis is that there is a greater possibility of evaluating both the question and the conditions essential for answering it.

The heart of the matter is this: historical materialism |

1

will be applicable to the development of "primitive" social formations and their study will become truly scientific when, and only when, two conditions are on the way to being fulfilled: (1) When the results of ethnographic research and the ideas of bourgeois ethnology are themselves being critically transformed into their very "subject"; and (2) when the fundamental concepts of historical materialism are themselves being transformed in such a way as to produce exact studies in a new and specific field.

These two conditions cannot be disassociated and refer to a single theoretical operation. It is not enough to uncritically accept ethnological or even ethnographic "data," thus attributing to knowledge a purpose which often proves to be illusory or ideological. No better results will be gained by the mechanical application to the results of ethnological investigation of the special concepts required to understand the capitalist mode of production. On the other hand, it is not enough to repeat the few clues left by Marx or the analyses of "pre-capitalist" societies undertaken by Engels unless these are developed further. Thus it is necessary to undertake really fundamental work from which our understanding of the principles of historical materialism, put to the test of their concrete consequences, will be enriched. These principles must be put to work rigorously, as shown in *Capital*.

Such an undertaking is bound to be a long one. The studies which follow make no pretense of completing it, but are designed in their different ways to launch it and to make a contribution to its progress.

Emmanuel Terray's first study is a critical examination of traditional ethnological theory starting from an historically decisive point: Morgan's work and its various interpretations, which continue the debate between materialism and idealism. Confirming Engel's judgment, the study shows that there has been a real retrogression from the materialism of *Ancient Society*. To forget or misrepresent a book has meant to "forget" the essential question of the material modes of production, yet to ignore them makes the history of any human society unintelligible.

The second study shows the signs of a changing climate by analyzing Claude Meillassoux's *Anthropologie économique des Gouro de Côte d'Ivoire* (Mouton, 1964). This may not be the first meeting between anthropological research and the concepts of historical materialism, but it is certainly the first to have treated this meeting rigorously. Meillassoux's results make it possible to suggest a few theoretical hypotheses applicable to a very definite form of social formation in the area of "primitive societies."

These two studies will have achieved their purpose if, with their help, the level of understanding they represent can soon be surpassed.

Acknowledgment

This work could not have been completed without the advice, criticisms, and suggestions of Alain Badiou regarding the first essay and of Etienne Balibar regarding the second. At the same time, the comments kindly made by Pierre-Philippe Rey on a first version of the latter made it possible for me to correct some errors and clear up many areas of imprecision. Finally, the ideas developed here have often been discussed with Harris Memel Fote, Marc Augé, Jean-Louis Boutilier, and Pierre Osmo and these discussions were most profitable for me. I here give thanks to all those I have mentioned.

—E.T.

Morgan and Contemporary Anthropology

Such is Marx's second reading: a reading which might well be called *"symptomatic"* (*symptomale*), insofar as it divulges the undivulged event in the text it reads, and in the same movement relates it to a different text, present as a necessary absence in the first. Like in his first reading, Marx's second reading presupposes the existence of *two texts*, and the measurement of the first against the second. But what distinguishes this new reading from the old one is the fact that in the new one the *second text* is articulated with the lapses in the first text. Here again, at least in the way peculiar to theoretical texts (the only ones whose analysis is at issue here), we find the necessity and possibility of one reading on two bearings simultaneously.

Louis Althusser, *Reading Capital*, p. 28.

Present-day anthropologists see Morgan as a strange dual personality. He is first of all the author of *Systems of Consanguinity and Affinity of the Human Family* (1871) and no praise is too high for him: for example, Claude Lévi-Strauss not only sees him as "one of the great forerunners of social-structure studies," [1] but also as the founder of social anthropology:

> The main feature of the development of social anthropology in the past years has been the increased attention to kinship. This is, indeed, not a new phenomenon, since it can be said that, with his *Systems of Consanguinity and Affinity of the Human Family*, Lewis Morgan's genius at one and the same time founded social anthropology and kinship studies and brought to the fore the basic reasons for attaching such importance to the latter.[2]

Unfortunately, Morgan also wrote *Ancient Society* (1877), and for this work he was very severely criticized. He committed the mortal sin of evolutionism, for which he is condemned without appeal by agreement among the most divergent schools of thought. Here are the views of Claude Lévi-Strauss on evolutionism:

> It is really an attempt to wipe out the diversity of cultures while pretending to accord them full recognition. If the var-

9

ious conditions in which human societies are found, both in the past and in far distant lands, are treated as *phases* or *stages* in a single line of development, starting from the same point and leading to the same end, it seems clear that the diversity is merely apparent. . . . Prior in date to the scientific theory of biological evolution, social evolutionism is thus too often merely a pseudo-scientific mask for an old philosophical problem, which there is no certainty of our ever solving by observation and inductive reasoning.[3]

Now let us hear Paul Mercier:

There is an implicit negation of the complex past of present-day primitive societies when the men who are their members are presented to us as our "contemporary ancestors." This was the title of a much later work of popular anthropology, but one of the passages from Morgan quoted above is in the same vein. . . . This incomplete view of history is connected, however indirectly, with those remnants of ethnocentric ideas mentioned in the previous chapter. At that time there appeared many ill-considered systems for putting human societies into hierarchies. These were merely reflections of the cultural vanity of the men of the nineteenth century who believed that they held the only key to progress. . . . However, it is in the field of methodology that the disadvantages of a systemic application of the theory of evolution become most evident. Reference has already been made to Morgan's distortions of facts and it should be added that when data were lacking he ventured on rash extrapolations.[4]

Thus Morgan, structuralist in 1871, had become an evolutionist in 1877. Such rapid mutations are rare in the history of ideas, and the phenomenon calls for investigation. Only a close examination of Morgan's thinking will serve to show if it is really marred by the incoherence of which he stands accused. It is my purpose to re-read *Ancient So-*

ciety, to study Morgan's language, to note not only what is said *in* that language, but also what is said *in spite* of it and even *against* it. Such an undertaking presupposes a scrupulous respect for the text, which is why I have quoted extensively. But since Morgan is once more on trial, this is the least of the safeguards he is entitled to expect.

1

I do not doubt that an "evolutionist" reading of *Ancient Society* is both possible and legitimate: Morgan himself explicitly acknowledged his debt to Darwin and said that it was Darwin's influence that led him "to adopt the conclusion that man commenced at the bottom of the scale from which he worked himself up to his present status." [5] It is easy to pinpoint *Ancient Society*'s borrowings from *The Origin of Species* and *The Descent of Man*— primarily, of course, the idea of evolution. To Morgan, the human species is not immutable, whether considered in its cultural and social or in its biological aspect; it is subject to evolution, progressing through a series of states each of which develops out of the previous state and carries within it the seed of that to follow; and this evolution is similar to that described by Darwin for the natural species. Such statements embrace both a theory of history and a theory of man. The theory of man: that he is one animal species among many. Morgan saw man, as did Darwin, as a species of animal origin and earliest man as scarcely to be distinguished from the savage beasts that surrounded him:

> Mankind may be traced by a chain of necessary inferences back to a time when, ignorant of fire, without articu-

late language, and without artificial weapons, they de-
pended, like the wild animals, upon the spontaneous fruits
of the earth (p. 536). . . .

Promiscuous Intercourse.—This expresses the lowest
conceivable stage of savagery—it represents the bottom of
the scale. Man in this condition could scarcely be distinguished from the mute animals by whom he was surrounded. (p. 507)[6]

Man's subsequent evolution did not entail a break with
this animal origin. Morgan did not admit to any discontinuity between the animal kingdom and the human kingdom; within each individual the cultural order and the biological order were indissolubly linked and reciprocally
determined. The size of the brain was a measure of intelligence:

The lessening volume of the skull and its increasing animal characteristics, as we recede from civilized to savage
man, deliver some testimony concerning the necessary inferiority of primitive man. (p. 507)

But exercise of the intelligence contributed to the growth
of the brain. Darwin wrote: "The habitual practice of each
new art must likewise in some slight degree strengthen the
intellect." [7] This was echoed by Morgan:

With the production of inventions and discoveries, and
with the growth of institutions, the human mind necessarily
grew and expanded; and we are led to recognize a gradual
enlargement of the brain itself, particularly of the cerebral
portion. (p. 36)

Recognition of this rigorous correlation between the
brain and the intelligence, between the organ and its function, thus makes it futile to use man's "mental" achieve-
ments to argue that there is a difference in kind between

the biological and the spiritual, between the animal and the human. The frontier between humanity and the animal no longer occurred within the human species, for Morgan vigorously asserted that it was a unity, both in space and time. Unity in space, for Morgan utterly condemned the "theory of degeneration," according to which only some varieties of the human species were worthy of the name of man while others, although originally human, had fallen back into animality:

> The theory of human degradation to explain the existence of savages and of barbarians is no longer tenable. It came in as a corollary from the Mosaic cosmogony, and was acquiesced in from a supposed necessity which no longer exists. As a theory, it is not only incapable of explaining the existence of savages, but it is without support in the facts of human experience. (p. 7)

Unity in time also, for to Morgan there was a rigorous continuity from savage to civilized man, and nowhere was there a break, a mutation which could mark the advent of a human order radically distinct from the natural order:

> We have the same brain, perpetuated by reproduction, which worked in the skulls of barbarians and savages in bygone ages; and it has come down to us ladened and saturated with the thoughts, aspirations and passions, with which it was busied through the intermediate periods. It is the same brain grown older and larger with the experience of the ages. (p. 59)

The unity of the human species and the human individual, the animal origin of man, the concept of the human order as part of the natural order, all were axioms for Morgan that were obviously inspired by Darwin.

If our species is one natural species among others, then human history becomes a moment in the history of nature, the result of the same mechanisms and subject to the same laws. In short, the concept of history is dwarfed by the concept of evolution. Historians see history as the work of man; Morgan saw it as a process of which man is the subject:

> The events of human progress embody themselves, independently of particular men, in a material record, which is crystallized in institutions, usages and customs, and preserved in inventions and discoveries. Historians, from a sort of necessity, give to individuals great prominence in the production of events; thus placing persons, who are transient, in the place of principles, which are enduring. The work of society in its totality, by means of which all progress occurs, is ascribed far too much to individual men, and far too little to the public intelligence. It will be recognized generally that the substance of human history is bound up in the growth of ideas, which are wrought out by the people and expressed in their institutions, usages, inventions and discoveries. (p. 311)

Man was not conscious of this "social travail" which was "the substance of human history":

> The institutions of mankind have sprung up in a progressive connected series, each of which represents the result of unconscious reformatory movements to extricate society from existing evils. (p. 58)

Morgan saw the history of the historians as an appearance masking an evolutionary development whose forms and modes were identical with those of natural evolution. We can easily perceive this identity by setting side by side Darwin's theory of the evolution of species and that of Morgan on human history.

With regard to the starting point of evolution, Darwin rejected the idea of a single origin, considering "all beings not as special creations, but as the lineal descendants of some few beings . . ." [8] Similarly, in Morgan's view:

> Original ideas, absolutely independent of previous knowledge and experience, are necessarily few in number. Were it possible to reduce the sum of human ideas to underived originals, the small numerical result would be startling. Development is the method of human progress. . . .
>
> Out of a few germs of thought, conceived in the early ages, have been evolved all the principal institutions of mankind. (p. 59)

Darwin considered that evolution was continuous and proceeded by the accumulation of innumerable minor variations:

> Natural selection acts only by the preservation and accumulation of small inherited modifications, each profitable to the preserved being; and as modern geology has almost banished such views as the excavation of a great valley by a single diluvial wave, so will natural selection banish the belief of the continued creation of new organic beings, or of any great and sudden modification of their structure.[9]

In the same way, Morgan seeks to show

> how savages, advancing by slow, almost imperceptible steps, attained the higher condition of barbarians; how barbarians, by similar progressive advancement, finally attained to civilization . . . (p. ii)

Concerning the evolution of the family Morgan stated:

> It will not be supposed that these types of the family are separated from each other by sharply defined lines; on the contrary, the first passes into the second, the second into the third, and the third into the fifth by insensible gradations. (p. 394)

Darwin dismissed as secondary Lamarck's hypothesis that the origin of individual variations lay in a direct effect of the environment. He did not, however, trouble to identify their actual cause. Observing that similar variations can affect individuals in differing circumstances and different variations affect individuals in like circumstances, he concluded: "These considerations lead me to attribute less weight to the direct action of environmental conditions than to a tendency to variation arising from causes of which we are entirely ignorant." [10] In the same way, Morgan considered very secondary the part played by geographical determinism, which is to the social sciences what Lamarck's theories are to zoology:

> Differences in the culture of the same period in the Eastern and Western hemispheres undoubtedly existed in consequence of the unequal endowments of the continents; but the condition of society in the corresponding status must have been, in the main, substantially similar. (pp. 16–17)

Morgan left it to the historians to speculate on the historical beginnings of inventions or institutions, and on the precise circumstances in which they made their appearance:

> Whether the gens originates spontaneously in a given condition of society, and would thus repeat itself in disconnected areas; or whether it had a single origin, and was propagated from an original center, through successive migrations, over the earth's surface, are fair questions for speculative consideration. (p. 388)

Darwin saw natural selection as the real agent of evolution and individual variations were simply the material on which it operated. The same is true of Morgan: the development of the "arts of subsistence" conditions that of society because societies enjoying improved subsistence are thereby in better positions in the struggle for survival:

I think that the real epochs of progress are connected with the arts of subsistence which includes the Darwinian idea of the "struggle for existence." [11]

Natural selection takes place, however, even on the level of institutions, establishing those most favorable to the development of the species: this explains, for instance, why gentile exogamy replaced consanguineous marriage:

As intermarriage in the gens was prohibited, it withdrew its members from the evils of consanguine marriages, and thus tended to increase the vigor of the stock. . . . (p. 68) The organization into classes upon sex, and the subsequent higher organization into gentes upon kin, must be regarded as the results of great social movements worked out unconsciously through natural selection. (p. 48)

Particular situations may favor natural selection or, on the contrary, slow it down. It is known what Darwin thought of the effects of isolation: one species could not establish itself as distinct from another unless the variants from which it originated were isolated from the invariants and were thus obliged to cross among themselves. Emile Guyénot put it in modern terms:

Once a mutation has appeared in nature, it will only be able to maintain itself if special conditions of isolation counter the effect of amphimixis (crossing with the normal form) and favor the establishment of families or local racial groups of mutants.[12]

In the same way, Morgan thought that the different steps in human evolution are realized most perfectly in geographically isolated populations:

Another advantage of fixing definite ethnical periods is the direction of a special investigation to those tribes and nations which afford the best exemplification of each status, with the view of making each both standard and illustrative. Some tribes and families have been left in geographical isolation to work out the problems of progress by original mental effort; and have, consequently, retained their arts and institutions pure and homogeneous; while those of other tribes and nations have been adulterated through external influence. Thus, while Africa was and is an ethnical chaos of savagery and barbarism, Australia and Polynesia were in savagery, pure and simple, with the arts and institutions belonging to that condition. In like manner, the Indian family of America, unlike any other existing family, exemplified the condition of mankind in three successive ethnical periods. In the undisturbed possession of a great continent, of common descent, and with homogeneous institutions, they illustrated, when discovered, each of these conditions, and especially those of the Lower and of the Middle Status of barbarism, more elaborately and completely than any other portion of mankind. (p. 16)

On the other hand, Darwin believed that once a species was established, cross-fertilization gave it the best chances of survival:

The advantages of crossbreeding do not depend on some mysterious property inherent in the union of two distinct individuals, but arise from the fact that these individuals were in former generations subject to different conditions, or have experienced what is commonly described as spontaneous variation. In either case, the result is that their sexual components have become somewhat differentiated. . . . The damage caused by inbreeding is due to the lack of such differentiation in the sexual components.[13]

Morgan took up the same idea and applied it to societies:

There is a gain by accretion in the coalescence of diverse stocks which has exercised great influence upon human development. When two advancing tribes, with strong mental and physical characters, are brought together and blended into one people by the accidents of barbarous life, the new skull and brain would widen and lengthen to the sum of the capabilities of both. Such a stock would be an improvement upon both, and this superiority would assert itself in an increase of intelligence and of numbers. (p. 468)

The features which correspond are so many and so similar that it is tempting to close the investigation and conclude that Morgan's "genius" lies in having applied to human evolution the concepts Darwin developed to explain natural evolution. In the *Origin of Species* Darwin constructed a model of evolution as the accumulation of favorable variations under the pressure of natural selection and the struggle for survival; Morgan only transferred this model to the study of history.

Some indications should, however, give rise to caution about this interpretation. Firstly, the external evidence: the admiration in which Marx and Engels held Morgan's work. According to Emile Bottigelli, Marx read *Ancient Society* between December 1880 and March 1881 and took no less than 98 pages of notes.[14] In a letter to Kautsky dated February 16, 1884, Engels had this to say of *Ancient Society*:

There exists a definitive book on the origins of society, as definitive as Darwin's work for biology, and it is, naturally, again Marx who has discovered it: it is Morgan, *Ancient Society*, 1877. Marx spoke to me of it but I had other matters on my mind and he did not return to the subject. This surely pleased him for I can see by his very detailed extracts that he wanted to introduce it to the Germans himself. Within the limits set by his subject, Morgan spontaneously discovered Marx' materialist conception of history, and his conclusions with regard to present-day society are absolutely communist postulates. The Roman and Greek gens is for the first time fully explained by those of savages, especially the American Indians, and this gives a solid base to primitive history.[15]

Engels's enthusiasm had not declined seven years later. In the preface to the fourth edition of *The Origin of the Family*, he referred to Morgan's discovery of the Iroquois gens:

> This rediscovery of the primitive matriarchal gens as the earlier stage of the patriarchal gens of civilized peoples has the same importance for anthropology as Darwin's theory of evolution has for biology and Marx's theory of surplus value for political economy.[16]

There could hardly be higher praise.

It is known, moreover, that after the publication of *The Origin of Species* many publicists tried to apply Darwin's concepts to human history and it is also known how forcefully Marx and Engels condemned these attempts. On June 27, 1870, Marx wrote to Kugelmann:

> Herr Lange, you see, has made a great discovery. The whole of history can be brought under a single great natural law. This natural law is the *phrase* (in this application Darwin's expression becomes nothing but a phrase) "the struggle for life," and the content of this phrase is the Malthusian law of population or, rather, over-population. So, instead of analyzing the struggle for life as represented historically in varying and definite forms of society, all that has to be done is to translate every concrete struggle into the phrase "struggle for life," and this phrase itself into the Malthusian population fantasy. One must admit that this is a very impressive method—good for swaggering, sham-scientific, bombastic ignorance and intellectual laziness.[17]

Engels wrote to Lavrov in the same vein on November 12, 1875:

If . . . a so-called naturalist allows himself to sum up the wealth and variety of historical evolution in one narrow, unilateral formula, "the struggle for life," a formula which can be accepted even in the realm of nature only *cum grano salis*, then the method contains its own condemnation . . . The essential difference between human and animal societies is that animals at most collect objects, while men produce. This single, but principal, difference is sufficient to invalidate the simple transposition to human societies of laws valid for those of animals . . .

To see history up to the present as a class struggle is enough to demonstrate the superficial nature of an approach that seeks to make this history into an almost undifferentiated "struggle for life." [18]

The conclusion now becomes inevitable: if Morgan's work had been nothing but the transfer of Darwin's biological concepts and methods to history, Marx and Engels would have condemned it as they condemned Lange's essay and the articles Lavrov submitted to Engels. On the contrary, however, they ranked Morgan's work with the greatest: they cannot have stopped at the obvious "evolutionary" interpretation. They read *Ancient Society* in an original way which enabled them to find in it something beyond the appearance of Darwinism. What was this something? Simply "the materialist conception of history discovered by Marx forty years ago." [19]

Such penetrating readers as Marx and Engels can be trusted: an alternative reading of *Ancient Society* is possible. Just as in the Middle Ages anyone who wanted to be heard on any subject had to express himself as a theologian, so at the end of the nineteenth century "transformism" became the universal language of the biological and human sciences. I shall try to show that by means of, and in spite of, this "transformist" language Morgan tried to work out concepts leading in quite different directions. I think these directions include those followed by social anthropology up to the present and others which it is still hesitant to follow.

2

What is Morgan's primary object, in two meanings of the word: what is the object he treats, and what is the object he seeks to achieve? His critics would have us believe that Morgan set out to draw a graph of human evolution divided into four parts: evolution of inventions and of "arts of subsistence," evolution of government, evolution of the family, and evolution of property. Each of these evolutionary processes was said to appear as a series of stages through which all human societies pass, have passed, or will pass. The fulminations of the critics fell upon this supposed project: we are told that to undertake such a project when so little material had been assembled showed excessive ambition; that it could only be done with "conjectural history" made up of reconstructions without objective proof; that it implied reducing the infinite variety of human progress to a single journey.

criticisms of Morgan

I believe these criticisms are based on a serious misunderstanding of Morgan's intentions, a misunderstanding that can be cleared up by the simplest examination of the text. In a word, it was not Morgan's purpose to describe the different stages of human social evolution, or to write a history of humanity, but to construct a *theory* of that history, that is, a system of concepts to make it possible to think it out scientifically. On the one hand, I shall try to show what concepts were proposed and, on the other, what epistemology, or concept of science, was the basis for these propositions.

Here it is necessary to make a distinction between the history of inventions and of the arts of subsistence, which embraces a succession of facts and a process of progress by accumulation, and the history of institutions, which, in each of its three branches—government, family, property —embraces the stages in the growth of an "idea" and constitutes progress by the development of original "germs of thought":

> As we re-ascend along the several lines of progress toward the primitive ages of mankind, and eliminate one after the other, in the order in which they appeared, inventions and discoveries on the one hand, and institutions on the other, we are enabled to perceive that the former stand to each other in progressive, and the latter in unfolding relations. While the former class have had a connection, more or less direct, the latter have been developed from a few primary germs of thought. . . .
> The facts indicate the gradual formation and subsequent development of certain ideas, passions, and aspirations. Those which hold the most prominent positions may be generalized as growths of the particular ideas with which they severally stand connected. (p. 4)

This explains the titles of the last three sections of *Ancient Society*: "Growth of the Idea of Government," "Growth of the Idea of the Family," "Growth of the Idea of Property." The terms "idea" and "germ of thought" should catch our attention: Morgan was not studying government, family, and property in their empirical being or their historical manifestations, but the organic growth of "ideas" which go through various successive "forms," following each other in a "sequence" of progress. It can be seen how carefully Morgan makes this distinction: On the one hand, the objects of his study are the "forms" of government and family—political and family organizations as they are given in reality and available for observation by the ethnographer; on the other hand, they are the "sequences" of development of the "idea" of government or the "idea" of the family, successions of real history as recorded by the historiographer.

With regard to "forms," Morgan, as has been seen, insisted on the need to study them where they have been able to mature freely, sheltered from all outside influences:

> It is essential to systematic progress in Ethnology that the condition both of savage and of barbarous tribes should be studied in its normal development in areas where the institutions of the people are homogeneous. . . .
>
> In no part of the earth, in modern times, could a more perfect exemplification of the Lower Status of barbarism be found than was afforded by the Iroquois, and other tribes of the United States east of the Mississippi. With their arts indigenous and unmixed, and with their institutions pure and homogeneous, the culture of this period, in its range, elements and possibilities, is illustrated by them in the fullest manner. (pp. 472–73)

One can see that what interested Morgan about the Iroquois was not their government as such, but the system in so far as it was the most perfect embodiment—Morgan says "exemplification"—of the "gentile" model. Examples of this form, especially in the Old World, are often confused or disturbed by the phenomena of diffusion, borrowing, and conquest. In the same way, Morgan distinguished the "forms" of the family from real families, empirically observable. He concludes his analysis of the "punaluan" family thus:

> Theoretically, the family of the period was co-extensive with the group united in the marriage relation; but, practically, it must have subdivided into a number of smaller families for convenience of habitation and subsistence. (p. 454)

His astonishing indifference to the problems created by rules of residence should be noted, for in the field it is the residential groups that constitute the primary data for observation.

Finally, Morgan answered McLennan, who wanted to reduce "systems of consanguinity" to a simple matter of terminology.

> A system of modes of addressing persons would be ephemeral, because all conventional usages are ephemeral. They would, also, of necessity, be as diverse as the races of mankind. But a system of consanguinity is a very different thing. Its relationships spring from the family and the marriage-law, and possess even greater permanence than the family itself, which advances while the system remains unchanged. (p. 527)

Here again, it is the terminology which provides immediate apprehension of the empirical reality. But a "system of consanguinity" cannot be the object of direct observations; to analyze it, it is necessary to know the "form" of the family and the rules of marriage. It is not the point of departure but the result of research.

Since the "forms" of government, or those of the family, are not identical with real political and family institutions, it would be a senseless operation to combine a "form" of government, a "form" of family, and a "form" of property in order to reconstruct a real society. Morgan did in fact recognize within real societies the possibility of survivals or anticipations: a dominant form of government or family corresponds to a given period but, here and there, this form may coexist with vestiges of a logically anterior form or with the embryo of a logically subsequent one:

> In speaking thus positively of the several forms of the family in their relative order, there is danger of being mis-

understood. I do not mean to imply that one form rises complete in a certain status of society, flourishes universally and exclusively wherever tribes of mankind are found in the same status, and then disappears in another, which is the next higher form. Exceptional cases of the punaluan family may have appeared in the consanguine, and *vice versa*; exceptional cases of the syndyasmian may have appeared in the midst of the punaluan, and *vice versa*; and exceptional cases of the monogamian in the midst of the syndyasmian, and *vice versa*. Even exceptional cases of the monogamian may have appeared as low down as the punaluan, and of the syndyasmian as low down as the consanguine. Moreover, some tribes attain to a particular form earlier than other tribes more advanced; for example, the Iroquois had the syndyasmian family while in the Lower Status of barbarism, but the Britons, who were in the Middle Status, still had the punaluan. (pp. 470–71)

A particular form only develops to the full when isolation protects it from external influences, but such test-tube experiments are rare in history. In fact, the organization of a given society at a specific time often needs to be explained by the phenomena of borrowing and diffusion:

The foreign elements intermingled with the native culture in sections of the Eastern hemisphere produced an abnormal condition of society, where the arts of civilized life were remolded to the aptitudes and wants of savages and barbarians. Tribes strictly nomadic have also social peculiarities, growing out of their exceptional mode of life, which are not well understood. Through influences, derived from the higher races, the indigenous culture of many tribes has been arrested, and so far adulterated as to change the natural flow of their progress. Their institutions and social state became modified in consequence. (p. 472)

It is even possible for fusion to take place between societies in very different stages of evolution. Morgan analyzed the social organization of the peoples of Northern India in the following terms:

> A civilized people, the Brahmins, coalesced with a barba-rous stock . . . [This] brought their two systems of consan-guinity into collision . . . resulting in a mixed system. The aborigines, who preponderated in number, impressed upon it a Turanian character, while the Sanskrit element intro-duced such modifications as saved the monogamian family from reproach. (p. 408)

Thus Morgan acknowledged the reality of the phenomena of survival and anticipation, of diffusion, of borrowing and fusion. He did not, however, dwell on them:

> The first sub-period of barbarism commenced with the manufacture of pottery, whether by original invention or adoption. . . . (p. 10)
> Whether the gens originates spontaneously in a given condition of society, and would thus repeat itself in discon-nected areas; or whether it had a single origin, and was propagated from an original center, through successive mi-grations, over the earth's surface, are fair questions for spec-ulative consideration. (p. 388)

I have already referred to the Darwinian sources of this neglect; but the delimitation of the object Morgan had set himself makes it easier to understand: the disturbances and the effects of contact described earlier are in the field of the historian seeking to give an account of the structure of real societies. They could be of no interest to Morgan, who was not trying to write history but to establish the theory of such a history.

Similarly, the "sequences" of progress, the series of suc-cessive "forms" of a single idea, should not be confused with the series of events studied by the historians. In the first place, Morgan allowed for the possibility that the transition from one "form" to another might follow different paths: starting from the consanguine family, the Australian system of classes and the punaluan family of the Hawaiians both led to a gentile organization:

> The germ of the gens is found as plainly in the Australian classes as in the Hawaiian punaluan group. (p. 441)

In the second place, the transition proceeds at different tempos according to the different societies or conditions in which it occurs. It is slower, for example, in conditions of isolation:

> Adopting the theory of a progressive development of mankind through the experience of the ages, the insulation of the inhabitants of Oceanica, their limited local areas, and their restricted means of subsistence predetermined a slow rate of progress. (p. 387; cf. p. 41)

Similarly, the rate of progress varies during the history of a single society; nor are the leaders always the same in the course of progress:

> Wherever a continental connection existed, all the tribes must have shared in some measure in each other's progress. All great inventions and discoveries propagate themselves; but the inferior tribes must have appreciated their value before they could appropriate them. In the continental areas certain tribes would lead; but the leadership would be apt to shift a number of times in the course of an ethnical period. (p. 39)

It is most significant that there is no *élan vital*, necessarily metaphysical, such as would compel a particular real society to progress from one "form" of government or family to another, and to go through all the steps in the "sequence" of progress. When all the component elements of an institution are present within a society, that institution may or may not appear:

The Iroquois were in five independent tribes, occupied territories contiguous to each other, and spoke dialects of the same language which were mutually intelligible. Beside these facts certain gentes were common in the several tribes as has been shown. In their relations to each other, as separated parts of the same gens, these common gentes afforded a natural and enduring basis for a confederacy. With these elements existing, the formation of a confederacy became a question of intelligence and skill. Other tribes in large numbers were standing in precisely the same relations in different parts of the continent without confederating. (p. 128)

History thus affords examples of stagnation when a society reaches a given form, stops, and becomes fixed in that form:

Australians possessed an area of continental dimensions, rich in minerals, not uncongenial in climate, and fairly supplied with the means of subsistence. But after an occupation which must be measured by thousands of years, they are still savages of the grade above indicated. Left to themselves they would probably have remained for thousands of years to come, not without any, but with such slight improvements as scarcely to lighten the dark shade of their savage state. (p. 385)

It is even possible to find examples of deterioration and regression running counter to the general flow of progress:

The destruction of the ethnic bond and life of particular tribes, followed by their decadence, must have arrested for a time, in many instances and in all periods, the upward flow of human progress. . . . (p. 39) Cases of physical and mental deterioration in tribes and nations may be admitted, for reasons which are known, but they never interrupt the general progress of mankind. (p. 58)

We have seen that Morgan's vision of history is not as rigid as might be suggested by some of his statements—those always quoted by his critics—about the worldwide uniformity of human development. Such statements really refer to the succession of "forms," not to that of events. It is worth repeating that it was not as a historian that Morgan was considering the movement of history, the phenomena of transition and of change. In his view the fact that a particular people had passed from one condition to another at a particular time could be explained by various, and often accidental, circumstances, and their analysis was not his field of research:

> Two families of mankind, the Aryan and Semitic, by the commingling of diverse stocks, superiority of subsistence or advantage of position, and possibly from all together, were the first to emerge from barbarism. They were substantially the founders of civilization. . . . (p. 38)
>
> Civilization must be regarded as an accident of circumstances. Its attainment at some time was certain; but that it should have been accomplished when it was, is still an extraordinary fact. (p. 563)

When Morgan was examining the transition from one "form" to another, he was not concerned with the various pathways followed by any particular society; he left such facts to the historians. His attention was focused on the structure of those entities between which the transition was made and the logical relationship connecting them to one another:

> The intermediate stages of progress are not well asertained; but, given the punaluan family in the Status of savagery, and the syndyasmian family in the Lower Status of barbarism, and the fact of progress from one into the other may be deduced with reasonable certainty. (p. 443)

We have seen that these "forms" and "sequences" are not in any way simple representations of empirical reality. How then can they best be defined? Morgan stated that their epistemological status was that of hypotheses constructed to explain the facts, and their validity was to be judged solely by their effectiveness: *but what is the criterion of their effectiveness if not empirical facts?*

> Having collected the facts which established the existence of the classificatory system of consanguinity, I ventured to submit . . . an hypothesis explanatory of its origin. That hypotheses are useful, and often indispensable to the attainment of truth, will not be questioned. The validity of the solution presented . . . will depend upon its sufficiency in explaining all the facts of the case. (p. 516)

It is, moreover, noteworthy that each of the forms studied was described as an organic whole made up of interdependent parts. Considering first the forms of government, here is how Morgan presents the different stages of gentile organization:

> The plan of government of the American aborigines commenced with the gens and ended with the confederacy, the latter being the highest point to which their governmental institutions attained. It gave for the organic series: first, the gens, a body of consanguinei having a common gentile name; second, the phratry, an assemblage of related gentes united in a higher association for certain common objects; third, the tribe, an assemblage of gentes, usually organized in phratries, all the members of which spoke the same dialect; and fourth, a confederacy of tribes, the members of which respectively spoke dialects of the same stock language. (p. 65)

Clearly interdependence was absolute only between the exogamous gens and the endogamous tribe, one of which could not exist without the other. Nevertheless, the four components constituted an "organic" series, a whole of logically linked parts. The same applied to the "forms" of the family. The syndyasmian and patriarchal families could be set aside as transitional stages and the three principal forms of the family—consanguine, punaluan, and monogamian—were then also organic unities. Each comprised three elements—a form of marriage, a form of family, and a system of consanguinity—which combined to constitute a system:

> What we know by direct observation to be true with respect to the monogamian family, its law of marriage and its system of consanguinity, has been shown to be equally true with respect to the punaluan family, its law of marriage and its system of consanguinity; and not less so of the consanguine family, its form of marriage and its system of consanguinity. Any of these three parts being given, the existence of the other two with it, at some one time, may be deduced with certainty. (p. 498)

On the other hand, the sequences in which the different forms of government and family follow each other are themselves "organic" series, their constituent forms linked by logical connections. Morgan wrote of the sequence of forms of government:

> The idea of organized society has been a growth through the entire existence of the human race; its several phases are logically connected, the one giving birth to the other in succession . . . (p. 390)

He was even more explicit about the sequence of forms of the family:

> The natural and necessary relations of the consanguine family to the punaluan, of the punaluan to the syndyasmian, and of the syndyasmian to the monogamian, each presupposing its predecessor, lead directly to this conclu-

sion. They stand to each other in a logical sequence, and together stretch across several ethnical periods from savagery to civilization. (p. 422)

The logical structure of these sequences made it possible to start from a given form and reconstruct what preceded it and what followed it. Morgan made the following statement on the punaluan family:

> Given the consanguine family, which involved own brothers and sisters and also collateral brothers and sisters in the marriage relation, and it was only necessary to exclude the former from the group, and retain the latter, to change the consanguine into the punaluan family. (p. 433)

From this it followed inversely that one could find the consanguine family using the punaluan as a starting point simply by adding to the latter marriage between consanguine brothers and sisters. Morgan, moreover, wrote in a text already quoted:

> The intermediate stages of progress are not well asertained; but, given the punaluan family in the Status of savagery, and the syndyasmian family in the Lower Status of barbarism, and the fact of progress from one into the other may be deduced with reasonable certainty. (p. 443)

It is most tempting to see in the successive forms taken on by an idea—the idea of government, of the family, of property—a collection of *models* in the sense in which Claude Lévi-Strauss uses the term; models which make it possible to conceptualize the particular sphere of social life under consideration. The sequences in which these forms succeed each other in their turn appear as the *transformation groups of these models*. In the present state of knowledge the interpretation of these groups in terms of origins should perhaps be regarded as secondary.

It is useful to recall how Lévi-Strauss defines the idea of structure. He begins by distinguishing structure from empirically observed social relations:

> The term "social structure" has nothing to do with empirical reality but with models which are built up after it. This should help one to clarify the difference between two concepts which are so close to each other that they have often been confused, namely, those of *social structure* and of *social relations*. It will be enough to state at this time that social relations consist of the raw materials out of which the models making up the social structure are built, while social structure can, by no means, be reduced to the ensemble of the social relations to be described in a given society.[20]

I showed at the beginning of this analysis that Morgan's forms and sequences meet the above requirements fully: they cannot in any way be confused with empirical reality. In his discussion of structure, Lévi-Strauss writes:

> A structure consists of a model meeting with several requirements.
>
> First, the structure exhibits the characteristics of the system. It is made up of several elements, none of which can undergo a change without effecting changes in all the other elements.
>
> Second, for any given model there should be a possibility of ordering a series of transformations resulting in a group of models of the same type.
>
> Third, the above properties make it possible to predict how the model will react if one or more of its elements are submitted to certain modifications.
>
> Finally, the model should be constituted so as to make immediately intelligible all the observed facts.[21]

The third of these four conditions is really covered by the first two. With regard to the other three, the texts already quoted seem to me to prove:

1. That the forms of government and family are logical wholes composed of interdependent elements, and thus satisfy the first condition.

2. That the sequences in which these forms succeed each other are surely transformation groups, since one can pass from one form to the other by logical deduction; this fulfills the second condition.

3. Finally, that the criterion for the persistence of a form is its fruitfulness or, as Morgan puts it,

> will depend upon its sufficiency in explaining all the facts of the case. (p. 516)

A "structural" interpretation of Morgan is thus possible. To be sure, Morgan's structuralism is inspired by biology rather than linguistics: underlying his thought is the image of the organism, not that of the language. It is true that Morgan's vocabulary does not include the *terms* model, structure, transformation group; on the other hand, the *concepts* of model, structure, and transformation group are indeed to be found among his theoretical weapons. In both *Ancient Society* and *Systems of Consanguinity and Affinity of the Human Family* the tools of structuralism are at work, though in his case they are applied to all phases of social reality. However, Morgan's concepts did not find adequate expression in language. It has already been pointed out that transformist language was all Morgan could use in the historical and ideological conjuncture in which he was situated; his thought had to be cast in a mold which was not made for it. It would be unwise to underestimate the difficulties this language produced for Morgan's thinking: the images which encumbered him—organism, species, origin, embryo, growth, evolution, graft, selection—clouded his vision and hampered any advance or diverted him from a course as yet only dimly perceived.

The fact remains that with the imperfect tools available to him Morgan skirted territory which anthropological thinking was not to rediscover for sixty years. Skirted? In fact, at the turning point of the analysis sometimes "words came" to Morgan and at such points one finds formulations of extraordinary resonance. Thus the following is not written by Radcliffe-Brown or Lévi-Strauss, as one might think, but by Morgan himself:

> In dealing with the structure of society, organic relations alone are to be considered. The township stands in the same relation to political society that the gens did to gentile society. Each is the unit of a system. (p. 234)

However, it is certainly not this "structuralist" interpretation that attracted Marx and Engels. In fact, Morgan's "structuralism," like that of his successors, was based on a positivist conception of science in which, to quote Alain Badiou:

> The theory is the model, experimentation consists of isolating the empirical correlate which materializes the model; the experimental apparatus [must allow] for a separating effect exhibiting an approximate realization of the form.[22]

As we have noted, Morgan was not trying to give an account of the structure of real societies, but to work out a science of history. To this end he eliminated what he believed to be impurities characteristic of the actual: borrowings, survivals, anticipations, stagnations, regressions. Thus he proceeded to an operation of abstraction which came down to filtering the essential from the secondary. He remained prisoner of an empirical ideology of knowledge, described as follows by Louis Althusser:

> The whole empiricist process of knowledge lies in fact in an operation of the subject called *abstraction*. To know is to abstract from the real object its essence, the possession of which by the subject is then called knowledge. . . .

The real: it is structured as a dross of earth containing inside it a grain of pure gold, i.e., it is made of two real essences, the pure essence and the impure essence, the gold and the dross, or, if you like (Hegelian terms), the essential and the inessential. . . .

Once this basic structure has been firmly grasped, it provides us with a key in numerous circumstances, in particular to gauge the theoretical status of the modern forms of empiricism which present themselves to us in the innocent form of a theory of models . . .[23]

Alain Badiou believes that Marx, on the contrary, believed that:

It is impossible to set a theoretical conception of history against real history defined by its very complexity—its empirical impurity. In Marxist epistemology the complexity is constructed according to the concepts of theory. . . . It is the proper task of a theory of history to give an account of the nature of real society.[24]

The reason for Marx's admiration of Morgan must, therefore, be sought in other aspects of Morgan's work.

3

If one can say that Morgan practiced a form of structuralism, it is not flat and immobile like the modern variety. Hear Claude Lévi-Strauss define the tasks of the latter:

It should also be kept in mind that what makes social-structure studies valuable is that structures are models, the formal properties of which can be compared independently of their elements. The structuralist's task is thus to recognize and isolate levels of reality which have strategic value from his point of view, namely, which admit of representation as models, whatever their type.[25]

Once these models are constructed, their formal properties are compared and analyses made of the transformations which make possible the passage from models at one
particular strategic level to those at different strategic levels. This is structuralism at dead level: all levels are regarded as strictly equal because the structures they exhibit
are all, and equally, the product of the unconscious logical
activity of the human mind. As Lucien Sebag says: "Logic
has primacy with regard to the different levels of social organization, which are manifested as so many realizations
of this logic corresponding to the various purposes of
man." [26] Since these are logical correlations and not real
processes, the transformations which make possible the
passage from one level to another are reversible; the system can be traversed starting with any one of its constituent elements. To put it another way, since a specific type
of transformation is characteristic of each society—this is
the famous "order of orders" of Claude Lévi-Strauss—the
study of a society can always begin at any one of its constituent strategic levels: whatever the chosen point of departure it will always be possible to go on from it to find
all the structures which correspond to the different levels.
The idea that these levels are a hierarchy and that one of
them is superior to the others from the point of view of ex-
plication is entirely alien to contemporary structuralist
theory, notwithstanding appearances and contrary declarations of intent. To quote Lucien Sebag once more: "To
the extent that thought is not a simple reflection of something which is not itself, no absolute value can be attributed to a particular type of social phenomenon in relation
to any others." [27] Moreover, such superiority would not
make sense for the structuralists: they never conceive of
the relations between the various levels in terms of effectiveness, determination, and reciprocal action; their pur-

pose is to discover formal correlations between structures: homologics, isomorphisms, symmetries, and inversions are the terms they use to describe these correlations. Society at its different levels thus appears as a system of mirrors reflecting back to each other their more or less distorted images. Such a conception leaves no room for events or changes: in relation to the structure these appear as foreign bodies, a sort of toxic substance to be eliminated on pain of death:

> Demographic evolution can shatter the structure but . . . if the structural orientation survives the shock it has, after each upheaval, several means of re-establishing a system, which may not be identical with the earlier one but is at least formally of the same type.[28]

It seems fair to describe as immobile a structuralism which relies on such formulations.

Morgan's thinking leads us in very different directions. We will attempt to show that his affirmation of both the interaction and the hierarchy of the various phases of social reality is the cornerstone of his thought.

We have seen that sequences of progress form so many *regional* theories of history. The problem is then to learn how these regional theories can be articulated to form a *general* theory. Morgan first set out to demonstrate the possibility of such a general theory, showing that he presumed the unity of the subject to be proven. We find here the theme of the unity of human experience, but the philosophical and moral overtones should not be allowed to obscure the epistemological function: it is in fact the fundamental postulate of social anthropology insofar as it sets out to be a comparative science and to establish general laws. This unity of human experience is, in the final analysis, a product of the unity of human thought:

Out of a few germs of thought, conceived in the early ages, have been evolved all the principal institutions of mankind. Beginning their growth in the period of savagery, fermenting through the period of barbarism, they have continued their advancement through the period of civilization. The evolution of these germs of thought has been guided by a natural logic which formed an essential attribute of the brain itself. So unerringly has this principle performed its functions in all conditions of experience, and in all periods of time, that its results are uniform, coherent and traceable in their courses . . . (pp. 59–60)

The human mind, specifically the same in all individuals in all the tribes and nations of mankind, and limited in the range of its powers, works and must work, in the same uniform channels, and within narrow limits of variation. Its results in disconnected regions of space, and in widely separated ages of time, articulate in a logically connected chain of common experiences. In the grand aggregate may still be recognized the few primary germs of thought, working upon primary human necessities, which, through the natural process of development, have produced such vast results. (p. 262)

To put it more precisely, human experience is produced by the interaction of three elements: man's primary needs, the primary germs of thought, and natural logic. The identity of these in space and their permanence in time are the basis and assurance of this unity. Primary needs are the raw material on which germs of thought work, guided by natural logic; inventions and institutions are the product of this work.

It is tempting to interpret this appeal to natural logic as an anticipation of the theses analyzed above, according to which structures would "realize" the logic of the human mind. Here, however, appearances are deceptive. To Lucien Sebag, who closely follows the linguistic "model," the logical activity of the intellect is the source of all forms and organizations. Both social relations and the models which represent them are products of the mind, and as such can be determined by it. Reality and structure are contrasted only as different levels of intellectual activity. To Morgan, on the other hand, the mind is no more than an instrument whose use is determined by the problems presented to it, by the pre-existent raw material upon which it acts. Thus, for Morgan to say that the human mind remains identical with itself through time and space does not imply any theory as to whether the phases of reality in which this mind operates are hierarchical or not, for the mind is neither producer nor organizer of these phases. In Morgan's theory this insistence on the unity of the human mind had but a single function: to affirm the continuity and homogeneity of history. Morgan firmly rejected the idea of an irreducible origin for so-called primitive societies. He might have agreed that several separate histories had coexisted since man's appearance on the earth and that the nineteenth century first saw them fused into a single world history. However, he would certainly have made it clear that these histories are all subject to the same principles: it is in this that he proves himself an evolutionist. Even if it seems to present-day thinkers that each regional history corresponds to a distinct concept and group of axioms, they would agree with Morgan that these different histories all form part of the same science, that the concepts and groups of axioms belong to a single theory. The distinction between civilized and primitive societies continues to appear under familiar disguises in our time—cold societies and hot societies, societies defined by structuralism or by hermeneutics, industrial societies and underdeveloped societies: this distinction still justifies the very existence of anthropology as a separate discipline. If this distinction were to make any sense in Morgan's system of thought, it would certainly be inside the scope of history and thus for history to account for. In this respect Morgan was in advance, not only of his own time, but of ours.

The singleness of the human mind thus establishes the possibility of a unitary theory of history. In particular such a theory involves the interdependence of the sequences of progress at each stage of their respective development. Considered synchronically, this interdependence is shown by the solidarity which, at any given moment, links the forms belonging to the different sequences. There is a sort of "transverse" correspondence between these forms which together constitute an organic whole. More precisely, each form occurs at the intersection of two structures: a diachronic structure, the network of logical connections linking the successive forms of a single sequence; and a synchronic structure, the system of correlations between different sequences that links forms realized at the same point in time. We have seen that the idea of sequence enabled Morgan to conceive the diachronic structure. What about the synchronic structure?

Here the basic concept is that of the "ethnic period," which Morgan defines as follows:

> The discussion of these several classes of facts will be facilitated by the establishment of a certain number of Ethnical Periods; each representing a distinct condition of society, and distinguishable by a mode of life peculiar to itself. . . . (p. 8)

Each of these periods has a distinct culture and exhibits a mode of life more or less special and peculiar to itself. This specialization of ethnical periods renders it possible to treat a particular society according to its condition of relative advancement, and to make it a subject of independent study and discussion. (pp. 12–13)

This definition should be given the widest interpretation: an ethnic period is not defined merely by a special way of life; but—as shown by the care Morgan took in placing each of the forms he studied at a particular point in the succession of ethnic periods—the ethnic period is the sum total of the stages reached by the development of the society in the various spheres of its social life. Morgan listed these spheres very early in his book, first distinguishing inventions and discoveries from institutions. Inventions and discoveries together comprised what could be called a "technical state." Institutions, on the other hand, were divided into seven categories: subsistence, government, language, the family, religion, house life and architecture, and property (p. 4). From this list Morgan excluded language from his field of study, since it was the subject of a special science; religion he dismissed with abuse which merited the sarcasm with which it was received; and finally, he left out architecture as no more than the material reflection of the forms of the family. Thus an ethnic period was basically a technical state, an "art of subsistence," a form of government, a form of family, and a form of property. The problem was to learn the nature of the relations linking these diverse elements and the corresponding spheres of social life—in other words, to define the structure of the ethnic period.

It can be said immediately that these relations are of three kinds: relations of *compatibility/incompatibility; functional relations,* operating within the limits set by the first; and *relations of expression,* themselves subordinate to the second. Within a single sphere of social life a form usually goes with a "discourse" explaining it. Relations of expression may also unite two spheres, in which case functional relations become merely the image of relations of compatibility/incompatibility. These we have seen to be those forms of family, government, and property whose logical wholes have interdependent constituent elements. It follows that the realization of one form in a particular sphere excludes: (1) The appearance of an element contradictory to the form in question within the same sphere, and (2) the realization of equally contradictory forms in neighboring spheres.

The most striking example of the first of these cases is the incompatibility between gentile organization and social inequality and privilege:

> Monarchy is incompatible with gentilism. . . . (p. 126)
>
> No analogy exists between a lord and his title, and an Indian chief and his office. One belongs to political society, and represents an aggression of the few upon the many; while the other belongs to gentile society and is founded upon the common interests of the members of the gens. Unequal privileges find no place in the gens, phratry or tribe. . . . (p. 208)
>
> Hereditary right to the principal office of the gens is totally inconsistent with the older doctrine of equal rights and privileges. . . . (p. 232)
>
> Under gentile institutions, with a people composed of gentes, phratries and tribes, each organized as independent self-governing bodies, the people would necessarily be free. The rule of a king by hereditary right and without direct accountability in such a society was simply impossible. The impossibility arises from the fact that gentile institutions are incompatible with a king or with a kingly government. (p. 259)

Similarly in the second case: since the nature of an ethnic period is the sum total of the forms realized in the different spheres of social life at a given stage, it obeys the laws of compatibility/incompatibility. These laws allow certain elements to coexist, making possible some of the survivals or anticipations mentioned earlier but entirely inhibiting the coexistence of others. In his criticism of a text in which Herodotus stated that the population of Massagetes lived under a system of sexual promiscuity, Morgan wrote:

> The Massagetæ, although ignorant of iron, possessed flocks and herds, fought on horseback armed with battle-axes of copper and with copper-pointed spears, and manufactured and used the wagon (*amaxa*). It is not supposable that a people living in promiscuity could have attained such a degree of advancement. (p. 439)

Incompatibility does not necessarily imply the complete exclusion of one of the conflicting terms; but it at least keeps them apart by restricting them to different spheres. Thus the family cannot become a significant unit of social organization within the framework of gentile society:

> Nothing whatever was based upon the family in any of its forms, because it was incapable of entering a gens as a whole. . . . (p. 233)
>
> As all the parts must enter into the whole, the family could not become the unit of the gentile organization. (p. 477)

Functional relations come into play within the framework thus created by relations of compatibility/incompatibility. We have seen that there exist "primary human necessities" (p. 262) and "necessary wants" (p. 118), and that institutions are responses to these wants:

> Every institution of mankind which attained permanence will be found linked with a perpetual want. (p. 98)

Exactly what are these wants? The gentile form is the political institution which best responds to the need for social cohesion. It

> was the instrumentality by means of which society was organized and held together. . . . (p. 61)
> Out of the necessities of mankind for the organization of society came the gens . . . (p. 330)

The phratry was born of the need for a stage intermediate between the gens and the tribe. It

> did not possess original governmental functions, as the gens, tribe and confederacy possessed them; but it was endowed with certain useful powers in the social system, from the necessity for some organization larger than a gens and smaller than a tribe, and especially when the tribe was large. (p. 90)

The tribal council responds to the need for cooperation:

> The council had a natural foundation in the gentes of whose chiefs it was composed. It met a necessary want, and was certain to remain as long as gentile society endured. . . . (p. 118)
> It developed upon the council to guard and protect the common interests of the tribe. (p. 119)

Under the Roman republic the need to integrate immigrants and strangers led to the establishment of the institution of patronage:

> The institution of the relation of patron and client is ascribed by the authors last named to Romulus . . . A necessity for such an institution existed in the presence of a class without a gentile status, and without religious rights, who would avail themselves of this relation for the protection of their persons and property, and for the access it gave them to religious privileges. (p. 334)

The institutions of confederation and of chieftainship were both called forth by the need for military security:

> A tendency to confederate for mutual defense would very naturally exist among kindred and contiguous tribes. . . . (p. 124)
>
> Under a confederacy of tribes the office of a general, "Great War Soldier," makes its first appearance. . . . The office sprang from the military necessities of society, and had a logical development. (p. 149)

Among family institutions, punaluan marriage tended to overcome the disadvantages of consanguine marriage:

> The transition from one into the other was produced by the gradual exclusion of own brothers and sisters from the marriage relation, the evils of which could not forever escape human observation. (p. 433)

It was the function of Turanian kinship terminology to extend and preserve social relations:

> In familiar and in formal salutation, the people address each other by the term of relationship, and never by the personal name, which tends to spread abroad a knowledge of the system as well as to preserve, by constant recognition, the relationship of the most distant kindred. (p. 397)

Roman terminology provided the basis for a code of descent:

> It was introduced by the Roman civilians to perfect the framework of a code of descents, to the necessity for which we are indebted for its existence. (p. 492)

These examples will suffice to show that the needs and necessities cited by Morgan had nothing in common with those which later provided the basis of Malinowski's theory: Morgan's necessities and needs were social, not biological.

If indeed Morgan's work involved some kind of functionalism, it was certainly without pretension and limited to two kinds of statement. First, Morgan stated that all lasting institutions are a response to social necessities; this was more in the nature of a working hypothesis than a completed theory. Second, he related a particular institution—or rather one element of a particular form—to a specific social necessity: the tribal council to the requirements of cooperation, chieftainship to defense, etc. But he was careful not to attribute to a particular social sphere a unique and permanent function throughout the various ethnic periods: he did not investigate the general function of kinship relations, juridico-political institutions, etc. The function of any one of these was seen in the part it played during an ethnic period, and it was in a way a "unique essence." Its part might vary from one ethnic period to another: it would not make sense to give it a general and unique definition. Morgan's functionalism was controlled by the social logic of the relations of compatibility/incompatibility described above, and was, moreover, sufficiently modest and flexible to avoid those comprehensive, tautological pronouncements which too often tempted later forms of functionalism.

Finally come *relations of expression:* a form may be reproduced in a "discourse," related in the way the sitter is to the portrait. Within the sphere of government Morgan accorded this kind of reflection to laws, and also to what would now be more generally described as the juridical superstructure of political systems: law translates the effective functioning of the system and is limited to codifying what is already customary, simply making it clearer and more rigorous:

> The earliest laws of the Greeks, Romans and Hebrews, after civilization had commenced, did little more than turn

into legal enactments the results which their previous experience had embodied in usages and customs. (p. 550)

Similarly, the system of consanguinity expresses the rules of marriage and the form of the family already practiced at the time of its adoption:

A system of consanguinity is not an arbitrary enactment, but a natural growth. It expresses, and must of necessity express, the actual facts of consanguinity as they appeared to the common mind when the system was formed. (pp. 512–13)

Finally, the whole sphere of property reflects both inventions and discoveries and the evolution of institutions:

The growth of property would thus keep pace with the progress of inventions and discoveries. . . . The customs upon which these rules of proprietary possession and inheritance depend, are determined and modified by the condition and progress of the social organization. The growth of property is thus closely connected with the increase of inventions and discoveries, and with the improvement of social institutions which mark the several ethnical periods of human progress. (p. 535)

To the three categories of relations between the spheres —those of compatibility/incompatibility, functional relations, and relations of expression—correspond the three types of *historical effectiveness*, three types of action of structures upon one another. In the first place, the existence of relations of compatibility/incompatibility makes it necessary to enquire into the relative weight of the different spheres. In fact, it is not good enough simply to state that two forms belonging to different spheres are incompatible. If the purpose is not only to comment upon the course of history, *a posteriori*, but also to forecast it, or at least to understand its mainsprings, then it is necessary to know which form will prevail and push aside the other when a confrontation between two incompatible forms is likely to occur. In other words, some sort of hierarchy must be established between the different spheres of social life; it must be decided which are *determinant*, which will decide the forms that can or cannot be realized, which will decide the position and effectiveness of each sphere in relation to the others.

Morgan's conclusion is known—it was what earned him the admiration of Marx and Engels: the determinant sphere is that of the "arts of subsistence." The successive arts of subsistence form the main basis of the periods of human history—that is, the division of history into ethnic periods:

> It is probable that the successive arts of subsistence which arose at long intervals will ultimately, from the great influence they must have exercised upon the condition of mankind, afford the most satisfactory bases for these divisions, [into ethnic periods]. . . . (p. 9)
>
> Mankind are the only beings who may be said to have gained an absolute control over the production of food; which at the outset they did not possess above other animals. Without enlarging the basis of subsistence, mankind could not have propagated themselves into other areas not possessing the same kinds of food, and ultimately over the whole surface of the earth; and lastly, without obtaining an absolute control over both its variety and amount, they could not have multiplied into populous nations. It is accordingly probable that the great epochs of human progress have been identified, more or less directly, with the enlargement of the sources of subsistence. (p. 19)

Further, the arts of subsistence were not regarded simply as "cultural traits," characteristic of a particular epoch.

They were regarded as the basis for defining periods because they set both the limits within which social life could unfold at a given stage, and the limits of social organization. By what means is this determinant role performed? In the first place, the arts of subsistence determine the extent of both familial and political communities. Morgan wrote of the appearance of the plough in agriculture as follows:

> The plough drawn by animal power may be regarded as inaugurating a new art. Now, for the first time, came the thought of reducing the forest, and bringing wide fields under cultivation. Moreover, dense populations in limited areas now became possible. Prior to field agriculture it is not probable that half a million people were developed and held together under one government in any part of the earth. (p. 27)

In the same way the requirements of subsistence determine the extent of family groups:

> Wherever the middle or lower stratum of savagery is uncovered, marriages of entire groups under usages defining the groups, have been discovered either in absolute form, or such traces as to leave little doubt that such marriages were normal throughout this period of man's history. It is immaterial whether the group, theoretically, was large or small, the necessities of their condition would set a practical limit to the size of the group living together under this custom. (p. 57)

Moreover, each art of subsistence corresponds to what Morgan calls a "mode of life" or a "condition," the requirements of which shape the social organization.

On the basis of a particular art of subsistence a given area can only maintain a limited number of people, and in order to cope with population increases the community must devise a process of segmentation which will enable it to divide without losing its cohesion; this is one of the significant features of gentile organization:

> New tribes as well as new gentes were constantly forming by natural growth; and the process was sensibly accelerated by the great expanse of the American continent. The method was simple. In the first place there would occur a natural outflow of people from some overstocked geographical center, which possessed superior advantages in the means of subsistence. Continued from year to year, a considerable population would thus be developed at a distance from the original seat of the tribe. In course of time the emigrants would become distinct in interests, strangers in feeling, and last of all, divergent in speech. Separation and independence would follow, although their territories were contiguous. A new tribe was thus created. This is a concise statement of the manner in which the tribes of the American aborigines were formed, but the statement must be taken as general. Repeating itself from age to age in newly acquired as well as in old areas, it must be regarded as a natural as well as inevitable result of the gentile organization, united with the necessities of their condition. (p. 105)

However, this very process makes it extremely difficult to set up a strong power covering a vast territory:

> A personal government founded upon gentes was incapable of developing sufficient central power to follow and control the increasing numbers of the people, unless they remained within a reasonable distance from each other. (p. 112)

Morgan also stressed the mobility which such communities owe to a mode of life based on fishing, hunting, and shifting cultivation; and the predominance within them of relations based on kinship. He commented as follows on the description of the ancient Germans given by both Caesar and Tacitus:

> The condition and mode of life of the German tribes, as described by Caesar and Tacitus, tend to the conclusion that their several societies were held together through personal relations, and with but slight reference to territory; and that their government was through these relations. . . .
>
> Caesar remarks that the Germans were not studious of agriculture, the greater part of their food consisting of milk, cheese and meat; nor had any one a fixed quantity of land, or his own individual boundaries, but the magistrates and chiefs each year assigned to the gentes and kinsmen who had united in one body as much land, and in such places as seemed best, compelling them the next year to remove to another place. (p. 370)

The introduction of agriculture made the city possible, and also the "political society" whose social units are no longer based on kinship but on place of residence:

> In the Upper Status [of barbarism], cities surrounded with ring embankments, and finally with walls of dressed stone, appear for the first time in human experience. . . . Cities of this grade imply the existence of a stable and developed field agriculture, the possession of domestic animals in flocks and herds, of merchandise in masses and of property in houses and lands. The city brought with it new demands in the art of government by creating a changed condition of society. (p. 264)

In the sphere of domestic relations agriculture also made possible the transition from the extended family to the restricted family:

> Improvement in subsistence, which followed the cultivation of maize and plants among the American aborigines, must have favored the general advancement of the family.

It led to localization, to the use of additional arts, to an improved house architecture, and to a more intelligent life. Industry and frugality, though limited in degree, with increased protection of life, must have accompanied the formation of families consisting of single pairs. The more these advantages were realized, the more stable such a family would become, and the more its individuality would increase. (p. 469)

The determining role of the arts of subsistence was reflected chronologically in the order in which changes affecting the different spheres appeared: the initial change always occurred in the arts of subsistence. Thus in setting out his table of correlation between ethnic periods and forms of the family, Morgan stressed that a particular form belonging to a specific period always extended beyond that period into the earlier part of the following period: to put it another way, any change in the arts of subsistence always preceded a change in the form of the family:

The consanguine and punaluan families belong to the status of savagery—the former to its lowest, and the latter to its highest condition—while the punaluan continued into the Lower Status of barbarism; the syndyasmian belongs to the Lower and to the Middle Status of barbarism, and continued into the Upper; and the monogamian belongs to the Upper Status of barbarism, and continued to the period of civilization. (p. 471)

The process of determination is not, however, limited to this negative action: its function is not simply to exclude this or that possibility; it also plays a positive role. It is important to understand the nature of this positive role. Morgan did not see an art of subsistence "engendering" a form of the family or a form of government. If this idea of origins is to be preserved at all costs, the source of a particular existing form must be sought in earlier forms within the same sphere. The sphere of the arts of subsistence is determinant but *not* creative; it poses the problems social survival depends on, and society must find a form of organization—form of family, of government, of property—which makes it possible to find the best solution for these problems. Morgan described spheres that had their particular content and structural laws, and were not created by the arts of subsistence; but they remain subordinate to the art of subsistence in a dual sense: first, by virtue of the laws of compatibility/incompatibility set out above, and then because it is the function of the forms realized within them to solve problems posed in the sphere of subsistence. To put it another way, each sphere has a specific content and specific structural laws, and comprises a combination of means by which society can ensure its own continuity as a society in the face of the difficulties presented by its environment. The functional relations referred to earlier enter at this stage.

Morgan stated that an institution was the solution of a problem; but he was careful not to use this method of analysis to establish a two-way one-to-one relationship between a series of institutions and a series of problems, the institutions solving the problems and the problems explaining the institutions. Such a procedure goes by familiar stages and is implicit in the concepts of many contemporary functionalists: all the problems which society must face in order to survive as a society are catalogued, and the social organization concerned is then broken down into as many institutions as may be considered necessary to solve these problems. Thus each institution is in a way left to confront its particular problem in a dialogue which excludes any third party, and society appears as a cluster of functions each independent of the others. The cohesion of society as a whole is lost in such a conception and the mythical image of a social organism is then conjured up to restore it. This organism is able to maintain its "equilibrium" through the vicissitudes of its history, able to invent "responses" to the problems posed by its environment, and to transform itself in order to "adapt" to changes in its milieu. The only unity between the various institutions is the extent to which they are all conceived to be the product of this super-organism or super-subject.

In spite of his Darwinian inspiration, Morgan made no concessions to this "biological" concept of society. He sought the factors that united the institutions constituting a social organization in their relations to one another—at the level of concrete problems. The various problems facing society are, in fact, closely linked to one another. The solution of problem A determines that of problem B and excludes that of problem C: all three are linked by logical connections which make it wrong to separate them, to treat each of them as if it were unrelated to the others. On the other hand, they stand in a hierarchy, or at least an order of urgency; major problems can be distinguished from secondary problems. The solution of the latter will be subordinate to that of the former, which will thus dominate the whole of the social organization.

It is important to note that such a hierarchy is not constant. Problems are posed in the sphere of subsistence but they are of various kinds: they may relate to the amount of manpower available to the organization of production and distribution, to the techniques used, to the distribution of wealth or the instruments of labor. The relative seriousness of the different problems varies in proportion to the degree of development of the arts of subsistence. It follows that it is this degree which determines which problem shall be dominant.

Once the dominant problem has been identified, the question is how and where it can be solved. There are a number of possibilities for each problem. An advanced society will overcome an obstacle by means not available to one less developed; in short, the nature and effectiveness of the means employed also depend upon the level of development of the arts of subsistence.

Finally, two factors determine the point at which a particular problem can be solved: the precise nature of the problem and the means employed for its solution. The same applies to the dominant problem: by determining these two factors the degree of development of the arts of subsistence also determines the point at which it can be solved. This point lies within one of several spheres of social life; it is this particular sphere which is regarded as dominant.

I shall take examples from Morgan. During the period of savagery and the lower stage of barbarism, the arts of subsistence were very unproductive, the amount of property available was limited, and scarcity was the rule:

> But the property of savages was inconsiderable. Their ideas concerning its value, its desirability and its inheritance were feeble. Rude weapons, fabrics, utensils, apparel, implements of flint, stone and bone, and personal ornaments represent the chief items of property in savage life. A passion for its possession had scarcely been formed in their mind, because the thing itself scarcely existed. (p. 537)

During that period man was the most precious commodity; more especially, he was the only available source of energy. It follows that social organization was governed by the process of production of men, controlled by the rules of marriage and kinship; in these circumstances the sphere of the family was dominant. Its role was not limited to the area of demography: the problems of social organization were solved within it. The matrimonial classes of the Australians took the place of political organization and for this reason the first chapter of Morgan's section on the "Growth of the Idea of Government" was devoted to these classes. On the other hand, gentile organization, which Morgan regarded as a form of government, implied laws of exogamy; it thus provided for the regulation of marriages. Given a particular degree of development of the arts of subsistence, it can be seen that any form, realized in any sphere, may perform several functions and solve several problems; it is worth repeating that Morgan did not regard the spheres as specialized and that on this point he differed radically from modern functionalists. In the same way, a transformation in the arts of subsistence would give rise to decisive social changes within the dominant sphere. This is why the punaluan family and the gentile organization came to replace the consanguine family as a man's marriage outside the circle of his immediate relatives produced a more vigorous and intelligent variety of man, a better human stock:

> The gens, originating probably in the ingenuity of a small band of savages, must soon have proved its utility in the production of superior men. . . . (p. 74)
>
> In the course of human progress it (the punaluan family) followed the consanguine family, upon which it supervened, and of which it was a modification. The transition from one into the other was produced by the gradual exclusion of own brothers and sisters from the marriage relation, the evils of which could not forever escape human observation. . . . (pp. 433–34)
>
> It affords a good illustration of the operation of the principal of natural selection. (p. 435)

The primacy of natural selection in the earliest period of history does not conflict with the role attributed to the arts of subsistence. The major importance of natural selection was, in fact, due to the inadequacy of the arts of subsistence, their limited productivity, and their uneven returns; the art of subsistence is determinant as much because of its inadequacies and insufficiencies as because of its positive traits, as much because of what it is not as because of what it is.

It was only at the end of the period of barbarism that, because of a vast increase in the production and volume of disposable goods, wealth and property replaced natural selection and, in Morgan's own terms, became the *dominant* forces in society and governed the public mind:

> The idea of property was slowly formed in the human mind, remaining nascent and feeble through immense periods of time. Springing into life in savagery, it required all the experience of this period and of the subsequent period of barbarism to develop the germ, and to prepare the human brain for the acceptance of its controlling influence. Its dominance as a passion over all other passions marks the commencement of civilization. (pp. 5–6)

How was this domination of property and wealth expressed? Their development was manifested qualitatively in the growing differentiation of productive activities, and quantitatively in the increasing volume of disposable commodities. Qualitative differentiation brought to an end the political homogeneity of gentile societies in which all members carried on the same activities. Divergent and even antagonistic interests appeared, requiring the establishment of rules and the introduction of arbitrators. On the other hand, as we have seen, the increase of wealth made possible the birth of cities where traders and artisans settled, and facilitated the creation of vast political units, the nations of the future. But difficult problems are posed by the life of cities and nations, problems whose solution requires the intervention of a specialized administration. On the other hand, the quantitative increase of wealth leads to its concentration in a few hands and to the appearance of social stratification. Property and administrative duties are the foundations of the aristocracy. Social mobility increased, there was migration to the towns and to especially fertile lands; while some tribes were dispersed, others received strangers onto their territory but refused them all political rights or security of stay: that was the origin of the Roman plebs. Finally, slavery became widespread:

> Equal rights and privileges, personal freedom and the cardinal principles of democracy were also inherited from the gentes. When property had become created in masses, and its influence and power began to be felt in society, slavery came in; an institution violative of all these principles but sustained by the selfish and delusive consideration that the person made a slave was a stranger in blood and a captive enemy. With property also came in gradually the principle of aristocracy, striving for the creation of privileged classes. (p. 351)

The combined effect of these changes was a proliferation of conflicts—between rival cities, between peasants and urban traders, between patricians, plebeians, and slaves; gentile organization, become in a way too narrow, no longer provided a framework for the solution of society's problems. Thus it vanished, yielding its place first to military democracy, then to territorial organization and to a state made up of three powers: the *basileus* or *rex*, heir to the war chief; the senate, heir to the council of chiefs; and the assembly of the people, described by Morgan as follows:

> The growth of property tended to the establishment of the popular assembly, as a third power in gentile society, for the protection of personal rights and as a shield against the encroachments of the council of chiefs, and of the military commander. (p. 325)

Returning to the family, the development of wealth made the monogamous family both possible and necessary. Herds and permanently cultivated fields were a sort of axis about which the family revolved. Once man had more goods he wished to leave them to his own children and to exclude all other relations.

> Since the labor of the father and his children became incorporated more and more with the land, with the production of domestic animals, and with the creation of merchandise, it would not only tend to individualize the family, now monogamian, but also to suggest the superior claims of children to the inheritance of the property they had assisted in creating. Before lands were cultivated, flocks and herds would naturally fall under the joint ownership of persons united in a group, on a basis of kin, for subsistence. Agnatic inheritance would be apt to assert itself in this condition of things. But when lands had become the subject of property, and allotments to individuals had resulted in individual ownership, the third great rule of inheritance, which gave the property to the children of the deceased owner, was certain to supervene upon agnatic inheritance. (p. 553)

Thus it was the growth of wealth and the passions it aroused that led, on the one hand, to the transition from matrilineal descent to patrilineal descent, and, on the other hand, to the advent of monogamy as the only way of avoiding any uncertainty in the matter of paternity:

> The growth of property and the desire for its transmission to children was, in reality, the moving power which

brought in monogamy to insure legitimate heirs, and to limit their number to the actual progeny of the married pair. (p. 485)

These examples should suffice to illustrate the operation of the dominance of one sphere of social life over the other; they also allow a precise distinction to be made between determination and domination. Louis Althusser has shown how important this distinction is in Marxist theory, and it is our contention that it is just as necessary for an understanding of Morgan's thought. How are these two forms of efficacy articulated? The determinant sphere sets limits, creates certain possibilities, and excludes others; it also decides which sphere shall be dominant, which in its turn governs over the social organization. During the earlier part of history the arts of subsistence played the determinant role; it was only from the middle stage of barbarism on that the dominant and determinant functions began to operate directly upon the creation of forms of government and family: one may say that at that stage they were both determinant and dominant. Their effect had to pass a certain threshold before they could perform the dual role; before they reached that threshold they were certainly determinant, but the dominant function was performed by other spheres of social life, especially that of the family. This comes down to the fundamental Marxist thesis: the level of development of the arts of subsistence determines which sphere of social life shall be dominant during the period under consideration.

The third and last type of efficacy is the action of a form on the language which expresses it. In certain circumstances the transition from one form of family or government to another leads to a corresponding change in its reflection. Morgan considered this reflection to have very limited autonomy, based solely on inert resistance to pressure from its model. For any change in the model to have repercussions on the reflection, the change would have to be above a certain level in both depth and extent. Thus the transition from the punaluan family to the syndyasmian was not adequate to overturn the Turanian system of consanguinity:

> The family represents an active principle. It is never stationary, but advances from a lower to a higher form as society advances from a lower to a higher condition, and finally passes out of one form into another of higher grade. Systems of consanguinity, on the contrary, are passive; recording the progress made by the family at long intervals apart, and only changing radically when the family has radically changed. (p. 444)

A brief recapitulation is worthwhile at this point. In the previous chapter we saw how Morgan developed the concept of *form*—forms of the family, of government, and of property—in order to analyze the different spheres of social life. Within each sphere these forms followed in an ordered *sequence* of progress. The forms realized in the different spheres at a particular time together constitute an *ethnic period* which is itself structured by the relations linking these forms to one another. These relations are of three types: *compatibility/incompatibility relations, functional relations,* and *relations of expression*. The forms act upon one another, but their effects are measured and shaped by the nature of the relations constituting the overall structure; each type of relation is to some extent the channel for a particular kind of action. As a cable *conducts* an electric current, relations of compatibility/incompatibility conduct the *action of determination,* functional relations conduct the *action of domination*, and relations of expression conduct the *action of the model on its reflection*. Thus the script has been written and the scene set, but how are the roles to be distributed? The arts of subsistence have a monopoly on this determination; their level of development at a given time decides which sphere shall be dominant during the period concerned; and each form is accompanied by a reflection it acts upon by means of direct causality, a causality limited only by the very inertia of the reflection.

This brief recapitulation seems to me sufficient to show how correct Engels was in finding in *Ancient Society* "the materialistic conception of history, discovered by Marx forty years ago." [29] It is well known how much inspiration Engels took from *Ancient Society* in writing *The Origin of the Family*. Morgan's arts of subsistence are, in fact, no different from Marx's productive forces; the ethnic period is the mode of production together with the juridical and political superstructures it has called forth. Both Morgan and Marx see the economy as determinant in the final analysis; both Morgan and Marx see that each sphere of the superstructure has its own internal logic and reacts to the action of the infrastructure according to this logic; finally, Marx found his own theory of ideologies in Morgan's systems of consanguinity. In the last text quoted, Morgan presented the family as an active element, changing with society, and the system of consanguinity as a passive element, adapting itself to changes in the family only after a delay. Marx made the following note in the margin: "The same is true of the political, juridical, religious, and philosophical systems in general." [30]

When he praised Morgan, Engels may have been more right than he himself realized. As stated earlier, Louis Althusser and Etienne Balibar were the first to demonstrate the decisive importance of the distinction between determination and domination in Marx's thought; we have tried to bring out the latent presence of this distinction in Morgan's work. Althusser and Balibar were also the first to illuminate the concepts through which Marx conceived of change and transformation in history, the transition from one dominant mode of production to another. In the last chapter I shall attempt to show that the same concepts were at work in Morgan's theory in various disguises.

4

A general theory of history requires not only a theory for each of the states through which mankind has passed, but also a theory of *transition* from one state to another, a theory of change. What has Morgan to offer us on this point?

First, it should be remembered that a form of family or government is a logical and coherent whole whose various elements are directed to the solution of the specific problems which a society faces during a given ethnic period. As long as the problems remain the same so do the solutions; in other words, no form contains within itself the seed of its own transformation. Thus Morgan stated that gentile organization was perfectly adequate to the requirements of social life during the final period of savagery and the beginnings of barbarism, and continued to exist in its own likeness as long as new facts did not modify those requirements:

> Its [the gens] nearly universal prevalence in the ancient world is the highest evidence of the advantages it conferred, and of its adaptability to human wants in savagery and barbarism. . . . (p. 74)

The Iroquois confederacy is an excellent exemplification of a gentile society under this form of organization. It seems to realize all the capabilities of gentile institutions in the Lower Status of barbarism; leaving an opportunity for further development, but no subsequent plan of government until the institutions of political society, founded upon territory and upon property, with the establishment of which the gentile organization would be overthrown. (p. 152)

This did not mean that gentile organization excluded all conflict or antagonism. Morgan's statement does not imply a theory of social stability, or a thesis concerning the necessary adaptation of the social organization to its surrounding environment; it cannot be used as evidence that Morgan was a forerunner of contemporary functionalism. On the contrary, an immanent and essential tendency to disintegration was characteristic of gentile organization, and it could not eliminate it without destroying itself. In fact, gentile organization was incapable of bringing together large numbers within a single political community; consequently, when demographic growth went beyond a certain point clans, phratries, and tribes were obliged to divide:

A constant tendency to disintegration, which has proved such a hindrance to progress among savage and barbarous tribes, existed in the elements of the gentile organization. . . . (p. 104)

New tribes as well as new gentes were constantly forming by natural growth . . . (p. 105)

Division was neither a shock, nor an appreciated calamity; but a separation into parts by natural expansion over a larger area, followed by complete segmentation. (p. 107)

Thus the process of segmentation follows from an antagonism inherent in gentile organization:

Romulus had the sagacity to perceive that a confederacy of tribes, composed of gentes and occupying separate areas, had neither the unity of purpose nor sufficient strength to accomplish more than the maintenance of an independent existence. The tendency to disintegration counteracted the advantages of the federal principle. (p. 288)

But it must be emphasized that although this antagonism was inherent in gentile organization, it did not constitute a threat to its existence. In fact, the organization of the new cells exactly repeated the organization of the parent cells; the number of units varied but their structure was constant. Thus in one movement segmentation both revealed and condemned the limits of gentile organization, and then reproduced and perpetuated these limits. Segmentation played a part not unlike that performed by periodic crises within the capitalist mode of production. On these Marx wrote: "Capitalist production seeks continually to overcome these immanent barriers, but overcomes them only by means which again place these barriers in its way and on a more formidable scale." [31] Etienne Balibar correctly added to this:

Thus the only intrinsic result of the contradiction, which is completely immanent to the economic structure, does not tend towards the supersession of the contradiction, but to the perpetuation of its conditions. The only result is the *cycle* of the capitalist mode of production . . .[32]

If the terms clan structure and gentile organization were to be substituted for economic structure and capitalist mode of production in this formula, one would have a very fair description of the meaning of segmentation in Morgan's work.

Thus neither Morgan nor Marx found a real contradiction within the forms of government or family—an antagonistic contradiction which would have prevented the maintenance of the status quo. In other words, forms are not capable of spontaneous evolution, and here the limits —or the superficial nature—of Morgan's transformism become particularly clear.

A form is a complete system closed in upon itself; it cannot, therefore, be assimilated into an organism capable of growing and transforming itself. The component elements themselves may become modified and give birth to new forms:

> It is evident that the council, the agora and the basileus of the gentes were the germs of the senate, the popular assembly, and the chief executive magistrate (king, emperor and president) of modern political society. (p. 261)

But each element evolves independently, and the evolution of the elements should not be confused with the evolution of the form. Mutation of the elements does not lead to mutation of the form but to its *disappearance*.

What then is the motive for change? Effective contradiction comes from *outside* to condemn to death existing forms and to impose social change: specifically, it comes from the sphere of the arts of subsistence, which we again find in the determinant role. Inventions or discoveries mark the beginning and the end of each ethnic period. The catalogue is familiar: fire and fish-eating, the bow and arrow, pottery, the domestication of animals, metallurgy, and the alphabet. Leaving the alphabet aside—Morgan gave no clue as to the importance he attributed to its appearance—all other inventions introduced either new sources of subsistence or new instruments of production. Anticipating arguments concerning pottery, Morgan wrote:

The manufacture of pottery presupposes village life, and considerable progress in the simple arts. . . . (p. 13)

The introduction of the ceramic art produced a new epoch in human progress in the direction of an improved living and increased domestic conveniences. (p. 14)

The only real and effective causes of change are these inventions or discoveries:

The most advanced portion of the human race were halted, so to express it, at certain stages of progress, until some great invention or discovery, such as the domestication of animals or the smelting of iron ore, gave a new and powerful impulse forward. (p. 39)

To put it more precisely, not only do inventions and discoveries create the possibility of change, they also make it necessary. Particular forms of family or government correspond to a specific degree of development of the arts of subsistence, and it is when the latter progress that the old forms are prevented from surviving and must give way. Such progress in effect raises problems which the old forms are no longer able to solve. Morgan gave the following description of the movement which led Ancient Greece from gentile organization to military democracy, and then to political society:

Under the influence of advancing ideas and wants the gens had passed out of its archaic into its ultimate form. Modifications had been forced upon it by the irresistible demands of an improving society; but, notwithstanding the concessions made, the failure of the gentes to meet these wants was constantly becoming more apparent. . . . (p. 222)

The gens, which had so long been the unit of social system, had proved inadequate, as before suggested, to meet the requirements of an advancing society. . . . (p. 223)

Property was the new element that had been gradually remoulding Grecian institutions to prepare the way for political society, of which it was to be the mainspring as well as the foundation. (p. 224)

The source of change thus established, it remains to understand its mechanism. As I have said, the form is a logically and coherently structured whole. This definition has as a first consequence: if a transitional form is understood to mean a whole in which some elements from ancient forms coexist, however uneasily, with some from new forms, then Morgan did not recognize the possibility of a transitional form. It is conceivable that between forms X and Z there may exist an intermediate form Y which is an unavoidable step on the road from X to Z; but this form would be coherent in itself and could not be considered only an aggregate of traits, some borrowed from X and others from Z. In this context it is appropriate to analyze military democracy; its main characteristic was the increased importance of the war leader within an organization which was still gentile:

> Under a confederacy of tribes the office of general, "Great War Soldier," makes its first appearance. Cases would now arise when the several tribes in their confederate capacity would be engaged in war; and the necessity for a general commander to direct the movements of the united bands would be felt. Introduction of this office as a permanent feature in the government was a great event in the history of human progress. It was the beginning of a differentiation of the military from the civil power, which, when completed, changed essentially the external manifestation of the government. (p. 149)

Morgan maintained, however, that this innovation did not change the essential nature of the gentile organization, and that military democracy was more the final variant of gentile society than a completely new form:

The spirit of the government and the condition of the people harmonize with the institutions under which they live. When the military spirit predominates, as it did among the Aztecs, a military democracy arises naturally under gentile institutions. Such a government neither supplants the free spirit of the gentes, nor weakens the principles of democracy, but accords with them harmoniously. (p. 220)

To recall that the form is a concept developed for the purpose of analyzing historic societies is surely enough to demonstrate the inanity of the notion of a transitional form. For transition is a historical fact, not a theoretical concept; it is of the order of reality, not of the order of thought. The concepts used so far—form, sequence, ethnic period, etc.—are clearly inadequate for thinking about the phenomena of transition; a new distinction is necessary for contrasting the organization with the form. It will be seen that this was implicit in Morgan's work.

This distinction parallels that which Marx made between a socioeconomic structure and a mode of production. Marx saw that some social formations existed in which structure could only be grasped with the concept of a mode of production. As Louis Althusser has written: "A social formation has a structure based on the combination of at least two modes of production, one of which is dominant and the other of which is subordinate." [33] Form and organization are linked in a similar relationship, so let organization be defined as a combination of social relations in a group of people at a given time. Organizations can be found at various levels and in various areas of social life: during a given ethnic period each of the spheres defined earlier will present a specific organization. On the other hand, the term "form" will be reserved to designate the concepts which enable us to conceive of the various existing organizations. A form, as we have seen, is a coherent system of institutions. Bearing in mind that phenomena of survival, anticipation, and diffusion play an essential role in the constitution of real societies, it appears that it is usually necessary to refer to several different forms in order to explain a given organization. To take a modern example, we can describe the economic organization of an underdeveloped country and list its characteristic features: the predominance of agriculture, the part played by agricultural exports, the influence of foreign firms, and, in many cases, the presence of a state sector. An analysis of this *organization* would require the use of four *forms* of economy: a subsistence economy, small-scale mercantile production, capitalist production, and a state-controlled economy. Several forms may apply to a single organization, and it is their interaction which makes it possible to comprehend the organization.

The example of a developing country was not selected by accident, for what is development but a particularly typical example of transition? It is this very notion of organization which will make it possible to conceive of the phenomena of transition; if we do not want to talk of a "transitional form," we can and should instead use the term "transitional organization." For a transitional organization can be precisely defined as the coexistence of several forms, no single one of which has been able to dominate or drive out the others. I have no objection to the proposition that any organization is the result of a combination of several forms. But in any stable period one of these forms exercises a hegemony and the others are subordinate to it. On the other hand, what is characteristic of transition is an antagonistic equilibrium between two forms, one of which is on its way out and the other on its way in. The instability of this equilibrium is indicated by the precarious and fluctuating nature of the dominance of one form over the other: as long as transition is in progress the two forms can change places and become alternately dominant and dominated until the balance finally tips toward a return to the past or a step toward the future. Etienne Balibar shows this very well when talking about a Marxist analysis of manufacture:

> Periods of transition are therefore characterized by the *coexistence* of several modes of production, as well as by these forms of non-correspondence [between judicial and political superstructures and the economic structure— E.T.]. . . . Manufacture is therefore never *one* mode of production, its unity is the coexistence and hierarchy of two modes of production.[34]

Suggestions of a similar kind are to be found in the study Lenin and Trotsky made of the phenomenon of the duality of powers in a revolutionary period.

I shall show that these analytic principles are precisely the same as those Morgan applied to phenomena of transition in the sphere of government and of the family. I shall take Morgan's description of the system of matrimonial classes among the Kamilaroi of Australia as an example in the area of family organization. In modern terms the Kamilaroi have a four-section system of the Kariera type, as defined by A. R. Radcliffe-Brown and Claude Lévi-Strauss. Morgan saw this organization as the result of the coexistence and articulation of two forms. The first and older of the two was that of classes: the Kamilaroi were divided into eight matrimonial classes, four male and four female. These eight classes were grouped into four sections, A, B, C, and D, each composed of one male and one female class; the members of each considered themselves brothers and sisters and did not marry each other. Intermarriage was prescribed between A and B on the one hand, and C and D on the other. If we accept the terminology proposed by Lévi-Strauss, the sections of the husband and wife are a *pair*, the sections of the father and his children are a *couple*, and the sections of the mother and her children are a *cycle*. If a man belongs to a given section his children will belong to the alternate section of his own couple, as in the following table.[35]

A *man of:*	*marries a woman of:*	*his children belong to:*
A	B	D
B	A	C
C	D	B
D	C	A

On the other hand, the gentile form is also found among the Kamilaroi: they are divided into six exogamous clans, which are themselves divided into two equally exogamous moieties. Moiety I includes the Iguana, Kangaroo, and Opossum clans, Moiety II the Emu, Blacksnake, and Bandicoot clans. A man belonging to any clan of one moiety may only take as wife a woman from one of the clans of the other moiety. Finally, the Kamilaroi practice matrilineal descent: a child belongs to the same clan, and hence the same moiety, as his mother.

How are the two forms articulated? In other words: what sections must the clans comprise in order to obey both the laws of descent and marriage associated with the system of classes, and those associated with the clan system? The answer to this question makes it possible to understand the family system of the Kamilaroi.

Morgan gave an answer based on the observations of Lorimer Fison, but it could also be deduced from the rules set out above. First, the question arises as to how many sections make up a clan? Matrilineal descent requires the mother and her children to belong to the same clan, but the rules of descent associated with the system of classes also require that a mother and her children belong to two different sections—so the clan must comprise members of at least two sections. On the other hand, marriage is pre-scribed between sections A and B and C and D, and they cannot, therefore, belong to the same clan; if they did, marriage within the clan would be possible and the rules of exogamy would be invalidated. Thus it is impossible for any clan to comprise three sections since all possible com-binations of three sections would include A and B or C and D. It follows that two sections are represented within the clan.

Which sections are they? We have seen that neither A and B nor C and D can be included in the same clan; on the other hand, all the following four combinations are possible: AC, AD, BC, BD. But it should be noted that since the moiety is exogamous neither A and B nor C and D can be simultaneously represented in the same moiety. If, for example, the first clan within a moiety were to be composed of sections A and C and the second of B and D, then the members of one should, or at least could, marry the members of the other and the moiety would cease to be exogamous. Further examination shows that the same would be true of all other possible distributions (AC-AD, AC-BC, AD-BC, AD-BD, BC-BD). It follows that all the clans in the same moiety must have the same composition.

Two possible solutions remain: either the clans of the first moiety comprise sections A and C and those of the second B and D; or else the clans of the first moiety com-prise sections A and D and those of the second B and C. A choice can be made between the two by applying the rules of descent. By matrilineal descent the children belong to their mother's clan; on the other hand, the rules of descent associated with the class system provide that a woman's children belong to the section alternate to the cycle of their mother: woman A has children C, woman C has children A; woman B has children D, and woman D has children B. Hence the first solution proves to be correct: sections A and C are in the clans of the first moiety, and sections B and D in those of the second. It is now easy to check that the other solution would be correct if descent were patrilineal.

The Kamilaroi organization as described achieved a perfect balance between the form of classes and the gentile form: it might be said to be perched on the ridge between two slopes. This is what Morgan has to say:

> The gentile organization supervened naturally upon the classes as a higher organization, by simply enfolding them unchanged. That it was subsequent in point of time, is shown by the relations of the two systems, by the inchoate condition of the gentes, by the impaired condition of the classes through encroachments by the gens, and by the fact that the class is still the unit of organization. (p. 54)

However, this organization was also a transitional organization, a moment within a process which we must now reconstruct. According to Morgan, the starting point was a simple dualist organization composed of two exogamous moieties which exchanged women. Two kinds of change subsequently affected it. First, each moiety divided into two sections, A and C for the first and B and D for the second: intermarriage took place between A and B on the one hand and C and D on the other. Thus the system of classes was established. In the second place, the members of each moiety were distributed into three clans, without regard to the sections to which they belonged, so that each clan included members of both sections of the moiety. From then on the clan system was operative and it is at this stage that the organization described above was to be found.

Why these successive rearrangements? Morgan regarded the system of classes as having the function of limiting the biological disadvantages of consanguineous marriage. However, insofar as the system only forbade marriages between brothers and sisters and parallel cousins it largely failed in its purpose:

> The organization into classes seems to have been directed to the single object of breaking up the intermarriage of brothers and sisters, which affords a probable explanation of the origin of the system. But since it did not look beyond the special abomination it retained a conjugal system nearly as objectionable, as well as cast it in a permanent form. (p. 56)

The appearance of the gentile form could then be explained as a further attempt to eliminate the same disadvantages. However, the persistence of the system of classes reduced or wiped out the efficacy of this attempt:

> Since marriage is restricted to particular classes, when there were but two gentes, one-half of all the females of one were, theoretically, the wives of one-half of all the males of the other. After their subdivision into six the benefit of marrying out of the gens, which was the chief advantage of the institution, was arrested, if not neutralized, by the presence of the classes together with the restrictions mentioned. It resulted in continuous in-and-in marriages beyond the immediate degree of brother and sister. (p. 55)

From a purely formal point of view the organization described earlier achieves a perfect balance between the system of classes and that of clans; it entailed no logical contradiction and could have functioned harmoniously over an indefinite period. In spite of this, it did not provide a satisfactory answer to the problem confronting the Kamilaroi, that of consanguineous marriage. And the process I have described could not have been achieved within it. According to Morgan, the problem could only have been solved by the complete elimination of classes—and the Kamilaroi were moving in that direction. At the end of his analysis Morgan pointed out an "innovation" which was a complete break with the logic of the system of classes:

> It remains to notice an innovation upon the original constitution of the classes, and in favor of the gens, which reveals a movement, still pending, in the direction of the true ideal of the gens. It is shown in two particulars: firstly, in allowing each triad of gentes to intermarry with each other, to a limited extent; secondly, to marry into classes not before permitted. . . . Each class of males in each triad of gentes seems now to be allowed one additional class of females in the two remaining gentes of the same triad, from which they were before excluded. (p. 56)

Thus it can be said that the study of a *transitional organization* is an analysis of the relations of domination or equilibrium possible between two *forms*. We shall see that Morgan applied the same method to the area of political systems. We can take as an example his descriptions of the political organization of Athens between the time of Theseus and that of Cleisthenes; and of the political organization of Rome between the reign of Romulus and that of Servius Tullius. During these periods Athens and Rome had passed from military democracy—the final variant of an organization dominated by the gentile form—to the organization Morgan calls "political" (after Sir Henry

Maine). For the sake of clarity we shall call it "statist." To summarize Morgan's thesis: during this transition the two forms coexist within an organization whose structure is formed by the relations linking them together:

> It will be found the two governmental organizations were in existence for a time, side by side . . . one going out and the other coming in. The first was a society (*societas*), founded upon the gentes; and the other a state (*civitas*), founded upon territory and upon property, which was gradually supplanting the former. (p. 309)

We have seen that both in Athens and Rome the development of production and the increase in the amount of available wealth played an effective part in the transformation. This was a dual process: groups based on residential location replaced those based on kinship, and social stratification began. Changes affecting the political regime were merely reflections of these two innovations. First, migrations and the breakdown of the ancient tribes forced society to make way for territorial units. In fact, they brought about the establishment of a class of persons who had broken their ties with the tribe or clan of their origin and who would thereby have been excluded from participation in political and religious life:

> From the disturbed condition of the Grecian tribes and the unavoidable movements of the people in the traditionary period and in the times prior to Solon, many persons transfered themselves from one nation to another, and thus lost their connection with their own gens without acquiring a connection with another. . . . All such persons, as before remarked, would be without the pale of the government with which there could be no connection excepting through a gens and a tribe. . . . Having neither gens nor phratry they were also without direct religious privileges,

which were inherent and exclusive in these organizations. It is not difficult to see in this class of persons a growing element of discontent dangerous to the security of society. (pp. 273–74)

Various institutions based on territorial location were gradually established to reintegrate this class into society. In Athens the first of these to appear were the *naucraries*, which, according to Aristotle, were initiated by Solon. But these were military and fiscal groupings and as yet played a minor part in the functioning of the society. The gentile form continued to be dominant:

> The most important event that occurred about this time was the institution of the *naucraries*, twelve in each tribe, and forty-eight in all: each of which was a local circumscription of householders from which levies were drawn into the military and naval service, and from which taxes were probably collected. The naucrary was the incipient deme or township which, when the idea of a territorial basis was fully developed, was to become the foundation of the second great plan of government. . . .
>
> Notwithstanding the great changes that had occurred in the instrumentalities by which the government was administered, the people were still in a gentile society, and living under gentile institutions. The gens, phratry and tribe were in full vitality, and the recognized sources of power. (pp. 269–70)

The reforms of Cleisthenes and the establishment of demes and local tribes reversed the positions of the territorial principle and the gentile principle; the former became dominant and the latter persisted only as a survival in minor areas of social life:

> As a consequence of the legislation of Cleisthenes, the gentes, phratries and tribes were divested of their influence,

because their powers were taken from them and vested in the deme, the local tribe and the state, which became from thenceforth the sources of all political power. They were not dissolved, however, even after this overthrow, but remained for centuries as a pedigree and lineage, and as fountains of religious life. (pp. 280–81)

In the second place, the accumulation of wealth was accompanied by its concentration in the hands of a few. Further, the creation and development of cities led to a great increase in administrative duties and posts, soon monopolized by this minority. A difference now appeared between rich and poor, one which justified Theseus's reform:

> But another act is ascribed to Theseus evincing a more radical plan, as well as an appreciation of the necessity for a fundamental change in the plan of government. He divided the people into three classes, irrespective of gentes, called respectively the *Eupatridae* or "well-born," the *Geomori* or "Husbandmen," and the *Demiurgi* or "artisans." The principal offices were assigned to the first class both in the civil administration and in the priesthood. This classification was not only a recognition of property and of the aristocratic element in the government of society, but it was a direct movement against the governing power of the gentes. (pp. 266–67)

This was the first official recognition of the aristocratic principle, or as Morgan put it, of the aristocratic "element." Did it affect the political system? To all appearances nothing changed: the three organs of military democracy—the war chief, the council of tribal chiefs, and the popular assembly—remained present in their own image. But in fact the aristocratic principle in a sense developed the first of these three and established what might be termed a fortress at the very heart of the basically democratic organization of the gentile system. Henceforth, what had been a harmonious mechanism became the scene of a sharp antagonism:

> Since the council of chiefs remained as a constituent element of the government, it may be said to have represented the democratic principles of their social system, as well as the gentes, while the basileus soon came to represent the aristocratic principle. It is probable that a perpetual struggle was maintained between the council and the basileus, to hold the latter within the limits of powers the people were willing to concede to the office. (p. 257)

The temporary domination of the aristocratic principle was manifested in the tyrannies; but, according to Morgan, these did not take root:

> The nearest analogues of kingdoms among the Grecian tribes were the tyrannies, which sprang up here and there, in the early period, in different parts of Greece. . . . But such governments were so inconsistent with Grecian ideas, and so alien to their democratic institutions, that none of them obtained a permanent footing in Greece. (p. 260)

Finally, a new form of government was set up: the democratic republic. The component units were henceforth recruited on the basis of place of residence; apart from this change, the republic preserved the essence of the gentile inheritance. Once the aristocratic principle was eliminated the republic became the coherent form which completed the process of transition in Athens:

> When the Athenians established the new political system, founded upon territory and upon property, the government was a pure democracy. It was no new theory, or special invention of the Athenian mind, but an old and familiar system, with an antiquity as great as that of the gentes themselves. Democratic ideas had existed in the

knowledge and practice of their forefathers from time immemorial, and now found expression in the more elaborate, and in many respects, in an improved government. The false element, that of aristocracy, which had penetrated the system and created much of the strife in the transitional period connected itself with the office of basileus, and remained after this office was abolished; but the new system accomplished its overthrow. (pp. 260–61)

While the causes and first steps of the transition were the same in Rome as in Athens, the outcome was different: it was not the position of the war chief that was besieged by the aristocratic principle, but the council of tribal chiefs—or rather the senate, which was its successor.

Under the constitution of Romulus, and the subsequent legislation of Servius Tullius, the government was essentially a military democracy, because the military spirit predominated in the government. But it may be remarked in passing that a new and antagonistic element, the Roman senate, was now incorporated in the center of the social system, which conferred patrician rank upon its members and their posterity. A privileged class was thus created at a stroke, and intrenched first in the gentile and afterwards in the political system, which ultimately overthrew the democratic principles inherited from the gentes. (pp. 288–89)

In Rome the aristocratic principle could not be dislodged from the bastion it had conquered, and Morgan saw all Roman history as a battle between it and the democratic principle:

The Roman senate, from its high vocation, from its composition, and from the patrician rank received by its members and transmitted to their descendants, held a powerful position in the subsequent state. It was this aristocratic element, now for the first time planted in gentilism, which gave to the republic its mongrel character, and which, as might have been predicted, culminated in imperialism, and with it in the final dissolution of the race. . . . Under the republic, half aristocratic, half democratic, the Romans achieved their fame, which one can but think would have been higher in degree, and more lasting in its fruits, had liberty and equality been nationalized, instead of unequal privileges and an atrocious slavery. The long protracted struggle of the plebeians to eradicate the aristocratic element represented by the senate, and to recover the ancient principles of democracy, must be classed among the heroic labors of mankind. (pp. 322–23)

The above analyses show us precisely how Morgan conceived the mechanism of social change. We have seen that diverse organizations succeeded each other both in Athens and Rome. At one time these organizations were dominated by the democratic principle and the gentile form— as in the Athenian military democracy and republic; at another the aristocratic principle was dominant—as in the case of the tyrannies; finally, the antagonistic principles were at times in equilibrium, as in the Roman republic. But forms are realized in institutions and principles operate through institutions. It will be noted that at the conclusion of the evolutionary developments described new institutions had come into being but very few ancient institutions had disappeared. In both Athens and Rome, clans and tribes survived in the form of religious congregations; the organs of power were those inherited from gentile society. What had been changed was the relative position of these diverse institutions. Those which had begun as minor parts of the whole eventually imposed their hegemony; others, which had been dominant, were relegated to the rank of survivals. Thus what is at stake in a process of transition is not so much the existence or the nature of institutions as their place in the political system and their relative importance. An institution is in itself merely a foundation: while apparently unchanged, it may acquire new attributes, sustain new relations, and play very different roles. Today it may be at the service of democratic power and tomorrow provide a base for the aristocracy. This is why Morgan was quite right in stating both that the consuls, senate, and *comitiae* of the Roman republic were in a direct line of descent from the war chief, council of tribal chiefs, and people's assembly of the gentile organization, and that there had been a complete break, even a reversal, between the gentile organization and the Roman republic. The preservation of elements does not prevent a mutation of the system; it merely facilitates the integration of its various states into a group of transformations.

This brings the discussion back to the idea of sequences mentioned in Section 2. At an extreme, two successive forms may be composed of the same institutions; in such a case it is the displacement of the dominant from one institution to another that constitutes the transformation from one form to another; hence the transformation from an organization dominated by one particular form to one dominated by another form. It is the strengthening of the role of the war chief that transforms the gentile organization into military democracy. Different institutions combine to constitute a form and different forms to constitute an organization; between them there exists a relation of domination parallel to that which was earlier described between the different spheres which combine to constitute an ethnic period. Enough has been said to show how fundamental the concept of domination was to Morgan's theory: in brief, it enabled him to conceive structure and events simultaneously—a necessary condition for a scientific understanding of history.

5

The re-examination of *Ancient Society* is now complete. It can be seen that I have restricted it to a purely internal critique. We know that the information available to Morgan subsequently proved erroneous or insufficient on a number of points. The political system of the Aztecs prior to the Spanish conquest bears little resemblance to his description. In the field of relations of kinship and marriage, the consanguineous family and group marriage have been relegated to the category of ethnological errors—neither history nor ethnography have produced any trace of them; the institutions and customs upon which Morgan based his argument for their existence can justifiably be explained quite differently. Morgan's assertions on original sexual promiscuity, on matrilineal descent antedating patrilineal descent, and his views about patrilineal descent itself are now regarded as very doubtful. But we have avoided reference to research carried out after the publication of *Ancient Society*: it is not so much Morgan's results that are of interest as his intentions, not so much the theses he put forward but the concepts and methods he used to establish them.

On these points the verdict is in his favor. With regard to intentions, I have shown that Morgan set out to elaborate a theory of primitive history. According to Claude Lévi-Strauss, Anglo-Saxon anthropologists define the object of their discipline as follows:

In the Anglo-Saxon countries, anthropology aims at a global knowledge of man—embracing the subject in its full historical and geographical extension, seeking knowledge applicable to the whole of human evolution from, let us say,

Hominidae to the races of today, and leading to conclusions which may be either positive or negative but which are valid for all human societies, from a large modern city to the smallest Melanesian tribe.[36]

Which of these two projects is the more audacious? It is absurd to reproach Morgan for his vast ambition. The study of so-called primitive societies will have to set itself a task of the same magnitude if it is ever to go beyond the stage of monographic description and classification. Here again one could say that what matters is not the dimensions of the project but its content, not the extent of the area to be explored but the methods used to explore it.

This brings us back to Morgan's operational concepts—form, sequence, ethnic period, arts of subsistence, determination, domination, reflection, transitional organization—as we have extracted them from the Darwinian ore in which they lay buried. These concepts define the range and meaning of Morgan's enterprise, and it is on them that he must be judged. Taken separately, some prefigure structuralism, others functionalism, and still others naturally find their place in the edifice of Marxism, as Engels so shrewdly observed. In this sense it is possible to detect in *Ancient Society* the starting point of all the paths which anthropological thought has followed up to the present. This very ambiguity gives Morgan's book its importance, and also makes it difficult.

But the different ways of reading Morgan that I have distinguished—the evolutionist reading, the structuralist reading, and the Marxist reading—are not of equal value. I believe we have moved from the most superficial to the most profound. In fact, when Morgan thought diachronically he thought in terms of evolution and used Darwinian language; when he thought synchronically he thought in terms of models and structures and his language prefigured that of Claude Lévi-Strauss. But when he overcame this ideological opposition between the diachronic and the synchronic, he set himself a worthwhile task and tried to think in terms of history; he then produced the concepts which form the backbone of his system, and they are indeed the concepts of Marxism. So Engels was not wrong in ranking Morgan among the founders of the science of history. Today Marxist researchers are faced with the difficult task of applying the categories and methods of historical materialism to the vast area of so-called primitive society—up to the present left to various anthropological ideologies—and of building up a science of those social structures not dominated by the capitalist mode of production. By its failures as much as by its successes, by its errors and confusions as much as by its discoveries, Morgan's book provides one of the best possible introductions to this new science.

Notes

1. Claude Lévi-Strauss, *Structural Anthropology* (Garden City, N.Y.: Doubleday & Company, Inc., An Anchor Book, 1967), p. 282.
2. Ibid., p. 293.
3. Claude Lévi-Strauss, *Race and History* (Paris: UNESCO, 1952), pp. 14–16.
4. Paul Mercier, *Histoire de l'anthropologie* (Paris: Presses Universitaires de France, 1966), pp. 54–55.
5. Quoted by Eleanor Leacock, Introduction to Lewis H. Morgan, *Ancient Society* (Cleveland and New York: The World Publishing Company, Meridian Books, 1963), p. Iiv.
6. All references in parentheses refer to the Meridian Books edition of *Ancient Society.—Trans.*
7. Charles Darwin, *The Descent of Man* (London, 1888), vol. 1, p. 198.

8. Charles Darwin, *The Origin of the Species* (New York: The Macmillan Company, Collier Books, 1962), p. 484.

9. Ibid., p. 105.

10. Quoted by Emile Guyénot, *L'Origine des espèces* (Paris: Presses Universitaires de France, Collection "Que Sais-je?," 1966), p. 56.

11. Quoted by Leacock, Introduction to *Ancient Society*, p. Iiv.

12. Guyénot, *L'Origine des espèces*, p. 89.

13. Quoted by Jean Leroy, *Darwin et la théorie moderne de l'évolution* (Paris: Editions Seghers, 1966), p. 57.

14. Emile Bottigelli, Introduction to Friedrich Engels, *L'Origine de la famille, de la propriété privée, et de l'état* (Paris: Editions Sociales, 1964), p. 10.

15. Quoted by Bottigelli in ibid.

16. Frederich Engels, Preface to the Fourth Edition, *The Origin of the Family, Private Property, and the State* (New York: International Publishers, 1942), p. 16.

17. Karl Marx, *Letters to Dr. Kugelmann* (New York: International Publishers, 1934), p. 111.

18. Karl Marx and Friedrich Engels, *Lettres sur le Capital* (Paris: Editions Sociales, 1964), p. 276.

19. Engels, Preface to the First Edition, *The Origin of the Family*, p. 5.

20. Lévi-Strauss, *Structural Anthropology*, p. 271.

21. Ibid., pp. 271–72.

22. In a personal communication to the author.

23. Louis Althusser, "From *Capital* to Marx's Philosophy," in Louis Althusser and Etienne Balibar, *Reading Capital* (New York: Pantheon Books, 1970), pp. 35, 36, and 39.

24. In a personal communication to the author.

25. Lévi-Strauss, *Structural Anthropology*, p. 276.

26. Lucien Sebag, *Marxisme et structuralisme* (Paris: Editions Payot, 1964), p. 149.

27. Ibid., p. 152.

28. Claude Lévi-Strauss, *The Savage Mind* (Chicago: The University of Chicago Press, 1966), p. 68.

29. Engels, Preface to the First Edition, *The Origin of the Family*, p. 5.

30. Quoted by Engels in ibid., p. 27.

31. Karl Marx, *Capital* (Moscow: Progress Publishers, 1966), p. 250.

32. Etienne Balibar, "The Basic Concepts of Historical Materialism," in Althusser and Balibar, *Reading Capital*, p. 291.

33. Louis Althusser, *Sur Lévi-Strauss*, unpublished manuscript.

34. Balibar, "The Basic Concepts of Historical Materialism," p. 307.
35. Claude Lévi-Strauss, *The Elementary Structures of Kinship* (Boston: Beacon Press, 1969), pp. 156–57.
36. Lévi-Strauss, *Structural Anthropology*, p. 353.

Historical Materialism and Segmentary Lineage-Based Societies

The appearance of Claude Meillassoux's *L'Anthropologie économique des Gouro* (Economic Anthropology of the Guro) may prove to be a turning point in the history of anthropology. Leaving aside Soviet ethnology, which has up to now developed in isolation, Claude Meillassoux is the first researcher raised on the concepts and methods of traditional anthropology who has ventured to apply the categories of historical materialism to a specific "primitive" society. It is true that such men as Meyer Fortes and Max Gluckman were influenced by Marxist thought; that, more recently, Peter Worsley approached the problems of cultural contact in a Marxist spirit; and that for some years there have been more and more declarations of intent concerning the timeliness of introducing the principles of Marxist analysis into ethnology. It is to Claude Meillassoux, however, that credit is due for going a stage beyond projects and programs and trying to test the fruitfulness of these principles in the field. Whatever criticisms I may have to offer, I should state at once that the study and understanding of the results established in *L'Anthropologie économique des Gouro* are necessary to any further progress by Marxist research in the area of the so-called primitive societies.

Claude Meillassoux wrote his book for two reasons: on the one hand, he wanted to use the Guro as a starting point for a description of the mode of production of segmentary and lineage-based societies;* and, on the other hand, he wanted to analyze the transition of this traditional mode of production to a new mode characterized by the development of commercial agriculture. The two parts of the work relate to this dual purpose: the first part —the first ten chapters—is devoted to the self-subsistence economy; the second—the last two chapters—is devoted to the changes which followed the colonial occupation, the introduction of commercial agriculture, and the advent of a money economy. Between the two parts one chapter is devoted to pre-colonial trade and exchange: it appears, therefore, that Meillassoux regards this trade and exchange as a sort of preparation for the transition from self-subsistence to commercial agriculture. But since it was one aspect of the traditional economic system—and because it was not only contemporary with it but complemented it—I propose to study it as part of the self-subsistence economy. I shall stop there: however interesting the chapters in which Meillassoux studies the colonial period may be, I think they are far less new and original than his analysis of the traditional economy.

---

* I borrow the idea of segmentary and lineage-based societies from current ethnological terminology. It is known that a lineage is a group of persons who are in fact or in fiction descended from a single male or female ancestor in either the male or the female line. At each different level the lineage can be divided into segments embracing persons descended from one or the other descendant of the founder. In a lineage-based or segmentary society, local groups—villages, districts, etc.— are constituted on the basis of membership in a lineage. The lineage or segment is the kernel of the local group, and the relationship between local groups is both antagonistic and complementary; there is no central political authority. I regard this notion as of purely descriptive value and use it only as such.

Claude Meillassoux describes the mode of production of lineage-based and segmentary societies as

> cultivation of the soil, self-subsistence, the use of very short-term production techniques and of human energy as the main source of power. (p. 89)[1]

I would immediately wish to make a point which is not merely a matter of terminology. I do not contest this formulation and recognize that many Marxist texts give legitimacy to Meillassoux's use of this concept of a mode of production. Nevertheless, to reduce it to the enunciation of a few general characteristics of "self-subsistence economies" is, in my view, a waste of its operational fruitfulness. The characteristics enumerated by Meillassoux do in fact adequately describe lineage-based and segmentary societies in general. To state that a combination of these characteristics is a sufficient description of the mode of production of such societies implies that they all have the *same* mode of production; this means abandoning any attempt to explain the great variety of social and ideological relations observed in such societies. In other words, such a statement means abandoning any attempt to apply historical materialism to lineage-based and segmentary societies; or, at best, using it only in considering the distance between them and "industrial" societies.

A brief re-examination of *Capital* is enough to show that the analysis of a mode of production is not to be confused with a general description of an economy. The concept of a mode of production is far more precise and exacting. It should be remembered that a mode of production is a three-part system: an economic base, a juridico-political superstructure, and an ideological superstructure. In the final analysis the economic base is the determining factor within this system and must, therefore, be

the point of departure for the construction of the theory
of the mode of production. This economic base is, in its
turn, a combination of a system of productive forces and a
system of relations of production. According to the most
generally accepted interpretation, Marx meant the term
"productive forces" to embrace all the material conditions
of production—raw materials, tools, machinery, etc.—and
the term "relations of production" to cover the relations
established between the producers in the course of their
work. The two systems could therefore be described separately and their association studied afterward. However, as
Etienne Balibar has shown,[2] productive forces and relations of production do not relate to two separate categories of "things," but are two aspects of one single "reality":
the economic base of a mode of production can be
defined as one in which two systems of relations serve to
combine the various factors involved in the process of
production, labor power, and the means of production—
subject and means of labor. In the first place, these factors
are involved in definite technical relations which constitute the structure of the process of production, seen as the
process of man's material appropriation of nature; the concept of productive forces refers to this first articulation of
the factors of production among themselves. In the second
place, these same factors are involved in definite social relations which constitute the structure of the process of
production, seen as a process of the social appropriation of
the product. Here we find relations of production which
allocate the agents and means of production, and the division of the product which follows from that allocation.
The various factors composing the economic base of a
mode of production can be characterized in two ways: on
the one hand, according to their *technical effectiveness*—

their part in material production; and, on the other hand, according to their *social effectiveness*—their part in the production of social relations. The process of production, which is the process in which they are combined, also presents this dual character. In short, productive forces and relations of production are two conjoint forms of one and the same process, bringing the same factors into play. The unity of these two forms is brought about in a specific manner within the process of production and it is this which determines and establishes the identity of a mode of production.

The following operations are therefore required in order to construct a theory as to the mode or modes of production operating in a given socioeconomic formation:

In the first place, an inventory must be made of the various labor processes carried out within the formation: there, social labor is divided into a certain number of divisions, and labor processes are developed in each of these divisions: a raw material is transformed into a product by the joint action of the labor force and the means of production and this operation is carried out according to a specific *mode of material appropriation.** In theory every branch contains as many labor processes, and thus as many modes of appropriation, as there are distinct categories of products: elephant hunting is not to be identified with deer hunting. In the second place, several different labor processes, and hence several different modes of appropriation, may lead from the same raw material to the same product if different techniques are applied simultaneously or alternately: the elephant may be shot down or trapped. The term here would be *concurrent* modes of production.

---

* In the following text the term "mode of appropriation" refers to man's *material* appropriation of nature.

Finally, each of these labor processes may be simple or complex. If it is simple, a single mode of appropriation is put into operation: trapping is a *simple process*. A complex labor process is divided into several phases which are in themselves simple processes, each carried out according to a different mode of appropriation: the cycle of agricultural work required for a specific product is a *complex process* successively bringing into play several distinct modes of appropriation which are then said to be *complementary*.

When such an enumeration is complete, it becomes possible for the labor processes observed to be classified according to the specific technical relations which have been forged between the different factors of production during the operation of the process. Moreover, each labor process takes place within a given set of social relations of production and implies a particular allocation of the means and agents of production. These relations of production determine the distribution relations of the product; an analysis of these distribution relations may, in turn, throw light on certain problems difficult to solve at the production level. Let us postulate a complex labor process composed of several simple processes, each of which entails a different division of the factors of production, whose outcome is a single product. By studying the distribution of this product it will be possible to discover the pattern of division which is dominant among the different patterns that followed each other during the process. Thus a study of relations of production is only possible through the enumeration and examination of relations of distribution. The labor process, together with the relations of production in which it is carried out, constitute the *process of production*. From here it is possible to proceed to the enumeration of the various types of production processes characteristic of the socioeconomic formation under consideration.

Production units enter into these processes of production as subjects or agents. The dimensions and structure of these production units are determined both by the forces of production and the relations of production. Each unit combines factors of production in specific quantities and is also structured by the totality of the relations between its constituent parts. One aspect of these relations is technical and is dependent upon the circulation of raw materials, energy, or information within the production unit. Another aspect is the effect of the relations of production within the unit. From the point of view of the labor force a production unit is defined by the *form of cooperation* on which it is based. In fact, as soon as a process of production requires the cooperation of several independent units of labor power, it implies a work organization, an allocation and a coordination of tasks and can, in brief, be described as a form of cooperation. The different elements of the labor force brought together in the production unit may simply be juxtaposed or they may operate as a single agent, a sort of cell. Thus we can distinguish the different forms of cooperation corresponding to the different types of production unit. Whatever these forms may be, any collective work entails some division of labor, however elementary, because the unity of the process necessary for the execution of a collective task requires that the functions of coordination and decision be performed:

> All combined labor on a large scale requires, more or less, a directing authority, in order to secure the harmonious working of the individual activities, and to perform the general functions that have their origin in the action of the combined organism, as distinguished from the action of its separate organs.[3]

It follows that forms of cooperation are necessarily allied to *managerial and supervisory structures* which arise from the technical constraints of the process and of the relations of production within which the process is carried out. Finally, the relations of production determine distribution relations. The structure of the production units thus determines that of the *consumption units*. This does not mean, of course, that the latter always coincide with the former: on the contrary, such an exact correspondence is undoubtedly exceptional.

Finally, the relations of production are "represented" in the ideological and political relations which result from the articulation of the elements of its superstructure on the economic base of the mode of production concerned. Particular superstructural relations are, in fact, a necessary condition for the operation of particular relations of production. The former are both an expression and a deformation of the latter. For example, to the extent that the social division of labor acts on the level of the economic infrastructure to create a hierarchy between direct producers and organizers of production, this hierarchy will require a political and/or ideological sanction, the nature of which will be determined by the nature of the relations of production which gave rise to it. In certain circumstances political or ideological manifestations may play a part in the actual establishment of the relations of production, as can be seen in the case of the feudal mode of production. Thus it is important to distinguish the managerial and supervisory structures, as they are given in the economic base of the mode of production, from the political and ideological authority relations linked to these structures but not identical with them.

The complete concept of a mode of production can be assembled by combining these approaches. It then follows that the concrete social relations which can be observed by the ethnologist have a complex three-fold causality. In the first place, they are the result of the combined effect of three stages of a mode of production. On the other hand, they may be caused by the interplay of several modes of production and their respective stages. It can at once be seen that they appear as a synthesis of multiple determinations which is, finally, realized in a variety of social forms. Thus, in the type of society with which we are concerned production units may present themselves as solely and explicitly economic groups, but they may also appear in the form of kinship "cells," circles of friends, age sets, cultural or religious associations, etc. The analysis of a socioeconomic formation is not complete until these forms and their theoretical status and functions have been described.

This is what needs to be done to trace the constitution of a socioeconomic formation. The order of exposition should not, however, be confused with the order of investigation, which first requires the enumeration and identification of the various modes of production "present" in the formation under investigation. For this, the investigator has at his disposal indices which vary with the mode of production but which are determined by the instruments of labor:

It is not the articles made, but how they are made, and by what instruments, that enables us to distinguish different economic epochs. Instruments of labor not only supply a standard of the degree of development to which human labor has attained, but they are also indicators of the social conditions under which that labor is carried on.[4]

Of the various factors which combine in the production process, the instruments of labor are determinant because they give a dominant role to one or another of these factors. In other words, they make one factor the key to the combination of productive forces and relations of production: thus a study of this particular factor provides the starting point for the construction of the specifically different nature of the economic base of the particular mode of production. For the advanced capitalist mode of production Etienne Balibar has shown how the nature of an instrument of labor—the machine tool—has made the means of production—subject and means of labor—unite into the dominant element in the production process, and so has reduced the labor force to a subordinate position.[5] In the first analysis it is the unity of the means of production which distinguishes the capitalist production process from handicrafts, where the dominant element is the unit comprising both labor power and its instruments. Similarly, it should be possible to discover the dominant factor or factors in the production process of "primitive" socioeconomic formations through the study of their instruments of labor, and hence to construct a preliminary hypothesis as to the nature of the mode or modes of production concerned. It would then be possible to analyze the concrete social formations found in the field by the ethnologist and to begin to reconstruct the relations of production of which these structures are one "realization."*

Relations of production play the dominant role in the combination of productive forces and relations of production which forms the economic basis of a mode of production: what distinguishes one mode of production from another are its specific relations of production. When the

---

* These concrete structures also "realize" the political and ideological relations which "represent" production relations in the superstructure. This subject will be dealt with later.

reconstruction of the relations of production is complete, it should be possible to confirm or reject the initial hypothesis and to decide the number of modes of production operating within the socioeconomic formation.

Here I would like to temper the apparent severity of my opening comments on *L'Anthropologie économique des Gouro*. The great interest of this work is that, far from being restricted by the definition quoted earlier, Claude Meillassoux has most rigorously carried out the series of steps enumerated above. His book can thus be described as the first precise Marxist analysis of the economic sector of a "primitive" socioeconomic formation. This can be shown by following through the steps with him.*

IDENTIFICATION OF THE MODES OF PRODUCTION:
THE INSTRUMENTS OF LABOR

Our first task is to examine the instruments of labor used in the Guro socioeconomic formation. Claude Meillassoux describes them in the following manner:

> One . . . characteristic of traditional economies is the use of quasi-direct techniques of production: the product of labor is obtained almost directly. In other words, the producer interposes only instruments which have been made with few prior operations between himself and the object of his labor (the earth in the general sense of the term). (p. 90)

Indeed, on the one hand human labor is the principal, if not the only, source of available power. On the other

---

* To avoid confusion I would like to make it clear from the outset that I here propose only to list the modes of production "realized" in the Guro socioeconomic formation. I make no claim to construct a theory: far more research would be necessary before that task could be undertaken.

hand, producers' goods are of minor importance; social labor is almost entirely directed to the production of consumers' goods. The limited development of the productive force of labor is reflected in the fact that living labor outweighs accumulated labor in the value of the product. Looking at this from the qualitative point of view and leaving out the soil, which plays the part of an instrument of labor in both agriculture and animal husbandry, implements are generally tools or simple "manual machines" in the meaning given the term by André Leroi-Gourhan.[6] Marx analyzed the concept of a mechanical instrument of labor as follows:

> All fully developed machinery consists of three essentially different parts, the motor mechanism, the transmitting mechanism, and finally the tool or working machine. The motor mechanism is that which puts the whole in motion. The transmitting mechanism . . . changes its form where necessary, as for instance, from linear to circular, and divides and distributes it among the working machines. The first two parts of the whole mechanism are there, solely for putting the working machines in motion, by means of which motion the subject of labor is seized upon and modified as desired.[7]

In this combination the moment of transmission is dominant: thus Marx tells us that the tool is differentiated from the machine according to whether the function of transmission is performed by the human body or by a material apparatus. In one case the "program" of labor is inherent in the organism, in the other it is incorporated in an object. Guro implements can be divided into two classes: the first—knives, machetes, swords, etc.—are no more than the "operational part," and are simply a prolongation of the hand; the second—hoes, axes, etc.—have a transmission mechanism, usually based on the lever, which does no more than amplify and concentrate the force while the organism continues to perform the function of regulation and transmission. It should be added that their very simplicity makes most of these implements poly-valent—their nature does little to predetermine the use to which they will be put. Here the worker is the effective "site" of the labor process.

This analysis shows that the labor force is qualitatively and quantitatively dominant in the production process. The labor force participates in this process either as indi-viduals or as "collective workers"; and we have seen that collective workers can be organized in as many different ways as there are different forms of cooperation, these being at least partly determined by the implements used. In these circumstances the forms of cooperation observed can be used as indices to identify the mode or modes of production "realized" in the socioeconomic formation of the Guro.

IDENTIFICATION OF THE MODES OF PRODUCTION:
FORMS OF COOPERATION

In traditional Guro society time devoted to social labor was divided between six branches of production:

> Traditionally, economic activity was divided among hunting, the cultivation of crops, animal husbandry, food-gathering, and handicrafts. (p. 92)

The river villages also fished, as they continue to do today.

We shall now review these different branches and de-scribe the forms of cooperation appropriate to each.

Hunting

In this branch of the economy, where the soil is merely the object of labor, four modes of appropriation are used:

trapping small animals and hunting with bow and arrow or gun—both of which are individual activities—and trapping large animals and hunting with nets—which are collective activities (p. 94). In the first two the individual is the relevant production unit; of the third, trapping large animals, Meillassoux writes:

> The undertaking was launched on the initiative of a leader who spied out the animal and then assembled a team of ten to twelve men to set a trap on the track it was expected to follow. The trap consisted of a heavy pointed stake hung in the branches, and was brought down by the elephant as he came by. (pp. 98–99)

It appears that the entrepreneur assembles this team from among his fellow villagers, doubtless from his "brothers" and friends.

In the fourth case, hunting with nets, the production unit is the village (p. 93), or, more exactly, all the men of the village (p. 96). This unit is divided into three sections: two hunting groups, *beï* and *bebu*, and a group of beaters, who play a less important role. The form of cooperation at work in hunting with nets is determined by the use of a *collective* instrument of production, the net. Meillassoux gives little information about this instrument, but in the land of the Dida, immediately to the south of the Guro, two types of nets are found: the large net (*logae*), 100–150 meters long and carried by ten to fifteen men; and the small net (*sokuli*), 10–15 meters long and carried by a single man. The hunter can succeed only if the circle of nets and beaters is sufficiently wide, and this calls for the use of two to three large nets or at least twenty to thirty small ones. In either case a net cannot be used in isolation.[8] The same doubtless applies to the Guro. Meillassoux describes the social characteristics of this form of cooperation as follows:

Hunting is an intermittent activity with an immediate product. . . . [It] requires the discontinuous and temporary cooperation of a certain minimum number of men assembled for a single operation. . . . For this reason collective hunting is associated with a large but structurally diffuse territorial grouping, the village . . . (p. 123)

Cultivation of Crops

In this branch of production the soil is both the object and the instrument of labor. All the implements used—metal hoe, iron axe, machete, etc.—are individual implements of production (p. 105). Shifting or slash-and-burn cultivation is practiced (p. 106), which "requires cooperation between individuals of both sexes, which must be regular and consistent but varies in volume according to the work in hand" (p. 123).

In agriculture as many complex processes can be enumerated as there are finished products: the cycles of rice, yams, etc., will be considered as complex processes. Each of these cycles includes several stages:

—Preparing the ground; clearing the undergrowth, burning, banking (yams), enclosing (rice).

—Sowing (rice, maize, gumbo), planting (yams, manioc, taro), transplanting (bananas, and nowadays coffee and cocoa).

—Maintenance: weeding, tying plants to supporting sticks (yams).

—Harvest.

Each of these stages can be considered as a simple process.

In examining the division of labor and cooperation between sexes, it must first be noted that all agricultural activities require slashing and burning, which are men's work. Setting aside this preliminary stage, a distinction can be made among the complex processes:

—There are *masculine* processes, performed by men only: these include the coffee and cocoa cycles, with the exception of the assistance given by the women in harvesting.

—There are *feminine* processes, performed by women only: these include the maize, gumbo, manioc, and taro cycles.

—There are *alternating* processes, performed by men at certain stages and women at others. This applies to the rice cycle, where the men build the enclosure around the plot while the women sow, weed, and harvest the crop.

—There are *mixed* processes, where men and women work together at every stage: this applies to the cycle of the banana tree.

—There are processes which are *both mixed and alternating,* where certain stages are carried out by the men, others by the women, and still others by both together. In the yam cycle, the men bank and tie up the plants, the women weed and harvest, and both carry out the planting process.

This analysis may appear over-refined. The almost exclusively economic material presented by Meillassoux makes it impossible to go into greater detail here. However, this material does make possible distinctions among those processes which are solely masculine or feminine, those in which the sexes alternate or mix, and those in which men and women collaborate directly. We can also learn the relative importance of each and this may throw some light on the problem of the relations between sexes in a "primitive" socioeconomic formation. (It should be noted that among the Guro, the three major crops are rice, bananas, and yams, all alternate and/or mixed processes.)

Let us turn to forms of cooperation properly so-called. In general we find simple cooperation here: the assembled producers perform identical or analogous labor. The extent of the cooperation varies, however, between two extremes. The various simple processes enumerated above call for production units which differ in size and structure. Some processes consist of major operations—preparing the ground, seasonal harvesting—which have to be completed within a limited period. They require *extended* simple cooperation. Other processes—the lengthier ones—are mainly maintenance labor or day-to-day picking and require only *restricted* simple cooperation.

> Thus it can be seen how a single community breaks up into a number of work-teams and how within these even smaller teams can be observed. No team has the same agricultural tasks as any other, and they stand in a hierarchical relation according to the nature of the labor and the degree of cooperation they require, so that the teams are not merely added one to another but are dovetailed and interwoven. The smallest teams are made up of one or more monogamous or polygamous households and correspond to the domestic groups among the women; these perform more especially the tasks of crop maintenance, such as tying the yams, enclosing the rice paddies, weeding the grain crops, day-to-day picking. . . . A community is made up of several teams which assemble to undertake the more taxing labor and the tasks that need to be done quickly: clearing, banking, harvesting, etc. (p. 172)

I agree with Meillassoux in calling the production unit operating in restricted simple cooperation a *team* (pp. 172, 140, 153, 154, 159, 171), defined by its permanence and its small size. Another form of production unit corresponds to extended simple cooperation, and Meillassoux calls it the group (pp. 128, 138, 141, 153) or *production community*. It is distinguished from the team by its large size and intermittent operation.

The difference between these two forms of cooperation is not only one of size. From a technical point of view a *team* could be replaced by an individual: the production process would stretch over a longer period but the results would be the same. On the contrary, whether for reasons related to the production unit itself (as Marx said: "Just as the offensive power of a squadron of cavalry, or the defensive power of a regiment of infantry, is essentially different from the sum of the offensive or defensive powers of the individual cavalry or infantry soldiers taken separately . . ." [9]), or whether for reasons external to the unit, especially the limited period during which the task can be effectively performed, neither an individual nor a succession of individuals could perform the work of a *community*. Thus restricted simple cooperation and extended simple cooperation are really different in kind.

Finally, agricultural activities are complemented by domestic activities whose end product is edible. Domestic activities are the sole province of women and are carried out in restricted cooperation.

> The senior wife may be placed in charge of a considerable number of spouses, usually between six and eight, occasionally ten. The latter may sub-divide into several groups, each of the senior women taking a newcomer in charge in rotation. . . . The principle of strict rotation sometimes gives way to re-grouping by affinity. Each of these small groups of wives cultivates a common rice paddy; they have their own hearths, and each senior wife is in charge of a granary. (pp. 212–13)

Animal Husbandry

In this branch of the economy the land and the livestock are the principal means of production and are both the object and means of labor: the land plays the same part here as in agriculture. The labor input is relatively small because of the very rudimentary character of the traditional techniques of animal husbandry (p. 102). Part of this labor is invested directly in the process of production: it is mostly taken up in simple tasks of supervision. On the other hand, the production process can only be effective in the presence of "[objects which] do not enter directly into the [labor] process, but without them it is either impossible for it to take place at all, or possible only to a partial extent." [10] Thus an open, uncultivated space is left around the village so that livestock can graze freely, while barriers are erected around the "fields" and along paths to protect the crops. Here the labor process can be regarded as a complex process composed of two simple processes: one consists of controlling the course of a natural production process, the growing of livestock; the other consists of the management of the space in which this natural process takes place. Both can be performed equally well as individual work or in restricted cooperation. At the present time, owing to the colonial conquest and its effects, animal husbandry is of only minor importance; this no doubt explains the shortage of available information on the subject.

Fishing and Gathering

Fishing and gathering are occupations left to women and children and are performed in simple restricted cooperation:

> During the dry season the water level in the rivers falls and women gather in small groups to bale out the stagnant pools and collect the fish trapped in them. At certain times of year, especially in the short dry season, women and children collect armyworms, and in the wet season, snails. (p. 209)

Meillassoux describes the gathering of kola nuts as follows:

> Kola nuts are gathered between December and February, in the long dry season. Women and children go into the forest: the children climb the trees and the women carry the nuts. (p. 119)

He does not dwell further on fishing and gathering, whose social importance—except for the kola nuts—he says is diminishing:

> The gathering of caterpillars and snails by the women and children is of little social importance. . . . As for fishing, it concerns only that fraction of the population living in the river villages. The relations involved in these activities are impromptu and transitory and affect only a few individuals at any one time. (p. 92)

Handicrafts

The two forms of cooperation already observed in agriculture are found again here. Basketwork, cooperage, smithing, and weaving are masculine activities. Meillassoux writes as follows about the products of this work:

> Their manufacture does not necessitate cooperation, and a single artisan performs the labor in all its stages. (p. 190)

Here it is a matter of individual labor whose social effects will be seen to be similar to those of restricted cooperation. On the other hand, extended cooperation occurs in the construction and maintenance of huts—in terracing, building walls and roofs, collecting thatch, etc. (pp. 175, 178). What is most striking is the way in which agriculture predominates over handicrafts: the forms of cooperation imposed by the degree of development of the agricultural techniques are the very same as those used in handicrafts.

The latter do not lead to the appearance of new kinds of production units, and handicraft activities are carried out in the units "engendered" by agricultural production:

> In the traditional structure there is no specialist artisan, that is to say, one gaining the greater part of his living by such work. The artisan is always integrated within a social group built around agricultural activities; he is always first a peasant and secondly an artisan. (p. 189)

Enumeration of the Forms of Cooperation

We have found two forms of cooperation in the Guro socioeconomic formation; one of these is itself the result of combining two sub-forms.

1. The form of cooperation characteristic of hunting with nets, which can be described as *complex cooperation* and which is defined by the use of a collective work implement—the net. It requires a division of labor between hunters and beaters—one task performed by youths and adults, the other by children and old men—and this constitutes a first step, however elementary, in specialization.

2. The form of cooperation characteristic of agriculture, which can be described as *simple cooperation* in the Marxist sense of this term. This form is a combination of two sub-forms: (a) *extended simple cooperation*, practiced in major agricultural labor and also found in some forms of hunting (trapping large animals) and of handicrafts (building huts); and (b) *restricted simple cooperation*, practiced in agricultural maintenance work, and in gathering, fishing, and sometimes in animal husbandry.

3. Individual activities, such as hunting with the bow and arrow or gun, trapping small animals, manufacturing objects for common use, and sometimes animal husbandry.

Thus the branches and processes of production examined above can be classified in terms of the form of cooperation they bring about. Such a classification is shown in Table I.

The forms of cooperation characteristic of Guro society have been examined. To each of these there corresponds a specific production unit, and production units of the same type are "realized" in specific concrete forms. We must now examine these, which will in turn lead us to the identification of the social relations of production and the modes of production.

The Social Relations of Production Corresponding to Complex Cooperation: The Tribal-Village System

The men of the village together compose the production unit for hunting with nets (p. 96) and Meillassoux shows very clearly how the life of the village revolves around the axis of this activity. Hunting usually provides a key role in the location and relocation of a village:

> Traditions of origin are more often connected with hunting than with agriculture. In the tales we collected a secession is usually preceded by the discovery of an area rich in game, and the founder is often reputed to have been a great hunter. (p. 38) . . . Only a good hunter dared . . . risk settling on new land away from his brothers. . . . Tradition has it that most of the founders of present-day lineages were hunters, clearly showing the importance of this activity in the process of segmentation. (p. 95)

The territory of a village is basically defined by its hunting grounds:

Table 1

Branches of Activity and Forms of Cooperation

Form of cooperation	Hunting	Agriculture	Animal husbandry	Fishing	Gathering	Handicrafts
Complex cooperation	Hunting with nets					
Simple cooperation a) Extended	Trapping large animals	Preparing land, seasonal harvesting				Constructing and maintaining huts
b) Restricted		Sowing, planting, maintenance, & day-to-day gathering; domestic work	Minding livestock, building enclosures	Fishing	Gathering	
Individual labor	Trapping small animals, hunting with guns or bows and arrows		Minding livestock, building enclosures			Basketwork, smithing, cooperage, weaving

Hunting plays a major role among those factors which combine to establish and define a territory. When a village is settled the surroundings are explored by the hunters on their expeditions; as they blaze the trees to mark their return they outline the new domain. (p. 253)

It must be remembered that hunting with nets is the most important and effective form of hunting. Meillassoux stresses the importance of hunting as a factor in the disassociating of existing groups, but it seems highly probable that among the Guro, as among the Dida, groups will secede only if they are large enough to continue an activity as productive as hunting with nets. It also appears to cement the unity of the villages:

No form of cooperation linked with other economic activities, even with agriculture, is as extensive. Collective hunting with nets is an activity associated with the whole village and never with any smaller unit. It helps to create cohesion among lineages with often distant origins. . . . The disappearance of hunting with nets has certainly deprived Guro society of an integrating social factor and of an internal equilibrium that no other activity has so far replaced. (p. 89)

War was another factor exercising a considerable influence on the life and destiny of the village. It may cause surprise that this is mentioned in an investigation concerned with relations of production. And at first sight war cannot be considered an economic activity—Meillassoux thinks that it has few, if any, economic functions. His assumption that war is not properly speaking a productive activity is acceptable. However, in a social system in which "man is the only source of power" and where "the producer necessarily retains control of the economy and the goods it produces" (p. 90), it appears difficult to dispute that war has economic consequences. Marx admitted that wars had an economic function in the mode of production of ancient times, when land played a key role as object and means of labor and was the stake in most wars:

> Whatever obstacles may confront those who seek to work and appropriate it, the earth does not in itself obstruct the living individual seeking to relate to it in its inorganic nature as work place, instrument of labor, subject matter of labor, or source of sustenance. The only source of problems for a community is a different community either already in occupation or seeking to deprive the first community of possession. Thus war is the great collective duty and communal task required either to take possession of the material conditions of life or to defend and perpetuate that same possession.[11]

A Guro village or tribe went to war either to restore the balance of population disturbed by a murder or by the abduction of a woman, or else to increase the available labor force by acquiring prisoners: in both cases the purpose was to preserve or extend the labor force, which we have seen to be the dominant element in the process of production. In other words, wars are to assure the simple or extended reproduction of this dominant element. Thus it is logical that the "laws" of war forbid the killing of women. Here again war can be seen to have an economic function.

The general character of the social relations involved in war is very like that of the social relations involved in hunting with nets:* war too requires the division and coordina-

---

* Marx recognized the close relationship between hunting and war, as shown in the following text: "Linguet is probably right, when in his 'Théorie des Lois Civiles,' he declares hunting to be the first form of co-operation, and man-hunting (war) one of the earliest forms of hunting." (*Capital*, vol I, p. 334, n. 2.) This relationship is emphasized in the following comment made by André Leroi-Gourhan: "All possible forms of

tion of tasks that is complex cooperation. On the tribal level the social relations of the first are a mirror of those of the second, to the point of using the same terminology. The villages belonging to a tribe are divided into two groups, usually termed *beï* and *bebu;* the *doplazà* who directs the hunt corresponds to the *gulizà* who commands in war. As Meillassoux puts it:

> The organization of war determined the rather elementary structure of the tribe, in the same way that hunting with nets imposed a structure on the village, and similarly for other variants. (p. 232)

Thus what we may call the *tribal-village system* "realizes" the relations of production and relations in the superstructure which correspond to complex cooperation. The rules governing the allocation of the means of production and the distribution of the products reflect the characteristics of this form of cooperation. Hunting with nets requires the use of two types of means of production: a hunting ground and nets. A hunting ground is composed of all fallow village land; it is the collective property of the villagers, who use it freely. Members of the tribe to which the village belongs may also hunt on this ground, but are sometimes required to hand over part of their catch to the village. Meillassoux says nothing of the ownership of the nets: Among the Dida, where lineage is always co-terminous with hunting group, the large nets are the collective property of the lineage and the elders simply hold them in trust. Small nets belong to the minimal lineages. Among the Guro, the relations between lineage and hunting group are far more complex. In the savannah hunting groups are

---

violent acquisition of living creatures can be applied equally to war, hunting, and fishing." (*Milieu et techniques* [Paris: Editions Albin Michel, 1945], p. 71.)

recruited without regard to lineage; in the forest they are permanent moieties among which the village lineages are divided: hence lineage and moiety can be co-terminous only if the village contains two or at most three lineages. It does not, therefore, seem likely that the Dida rule applies, but none of the sources we consulted—works by Claude Meillassoux and by Louis Tauxier, articles by Ariane Deluz[12]—have settled the matter.

Two sets of rules relating to distribution correspond to the two types of relations between the tribal-village system and the lineage system. In the forest all hunters receive a share of the catch; the *doplazà* and actual catcher have a slight advantage over the rest. In the savannah each hunter keeps what he catches, with the exception of one paw which goes to the *doplazà* (p. 98). Finally, in some villages game is exchanged after the hunt between *beï* and *bebu*, who here seem to be the significant units. To conclude, it should be noted that where the distribution of the product of a hunt is the concern of all participants a *sharing* takes place. Meillassoux writes in a later article:

> The circulation of the product follows a short, diffused path: the collective product of the cooperative hunting group is divided and returned to each partner individually through the institution of sharing. Thus unlike what one observes in agricultural societies, there is no redistribution —that is, centralization of the product followed by a redistribution deferred through time—but instead it is done immediately and only once.[13]

All this shows how relations of distribution reflect the relations of production of which they are the obverse, but the difference between the savannah and the forest also shows how two systems of relations of production react upon each other; we shall return to this later. Finally, the sharing of the catch follows analogous principles (pp. 236–39). As for food, it is consumed in meal groups which we have yet to analyze.

Structures of direction and supervision are little developed in relations of production of this type. We have seen that the initiator of the hunt directs the expedition; for its duration he is obeyed unquestioningly, and he enjoys a modest advantage when the catch is distributed. However, his power is temporary, and it is most significant that any man in the village can be the initiator. Moreover, on the political level these structures of direction and supervision are not "represented" by permanent, institutionalized authority relations. Certainly, as Meillassoux writes:

> On the social level collective hunts provide the man taking the initiative with an opportunity to distinguish himself and acquire a temporary position of authority which might become confirmed by repetition. (p. 99)

But no formal privileges sanction this position of authority. As for the leader in war, he is sometimes chosen for his bravery, sometimes selected from among eminent men, but the role of war chief brings him nothing more than moral credit once the military operations come to an end. The conclusion is, therefore, that the political relations "realized" in the tribal-village system are profoundly egalitarian.

Social Relations of Production Corresponding to Simple Cooperation: The Lineage System.

It will be remembered that simple cooperation takes on two sub-forms, each of which will now be examined.

The *work-team* is the production unit engaged in restricted simple cooperation. It is "realized" in two different forms. Where the lineage structure is still strong, as for instance in Bazré (pp. 138–40), the work-team is formed within the family group and its membership can be described in terms of kinship; it is co-terminous with the segment of a lineage and any serious imbalance is rectified by the distribution of orphans and isolated individuals. With regard to this distribution Meillassoux writes:

> A functional reason for this sharing is . . . the concern to allocate to each [of the elders—E.T.] enough men for an effective work-team. (p. 100)

On the other hand, when the lineage structure is breaking down, as for instance in Duonefla (p. 159), the team is "realized" through the specific institution of the *klala*, in what one might call the *klala by pairs*. In this case, as Meillassoux records:

> Each team is . . . usually made up of two men. Pairing is based on affinity. Routine tasks in both field and plantation are more often performed by small groups than by those previously mentioned.* It is not a matter of an occasional alliance but of an agreement for the duration of the cycle of agricultural work. (p. 182–83)

Here we can see the features characteristic of production units based on restricted simple cooperation: limited numbers and duration.

The production unit engaged in extended simple cooperation is the *production community*. It is also "realized" in two forms, one when the lineage structure is intact and a second when it has broken down. In the first instance, it comes into being through a union of several work-teams, a union which follows the lines laid down by genealogy and which can be analyzed in terms of kinship. It is co-terminous with the lineage and in cases where the lineage is also

---

* This refers to *extended klalas*, which will be dealt with later.

the eating and residential unit, the production community has no special generic name; the term *dogi* is applied to this multi-functional unit. However, when the production community is not co-terminous with the eating unit—as in the Diazramo lineage at Bazré—it is called *nianawuo* (p. 128). Extended cooperation within the framework of the lineage is called the *bo*:

> Theoretically the *goniwuoza* (elder of the lineage) can call on the members of his *goniwuo* (lineage) to work together at clearing or other major operations in his fields. This often happens in the more integrated societies, but in their case the institution merges with the normal functioning of the community since the *goniwuoza*'s fields are theoretically common property. (p. 177)

The *bo* may be extended to include neighbors and allies, not thereby changing its nature but preserving the lineage as its kernel: what Meillassoux calls the communal *bo* seems to be simply an extension of the family *bo*.

On the other hand, if the framework of lineage has been weakened, the institution of the production community is again "realized" within the institution of the *klala*. Meillassoux analyzes the way in which the village of Duonefla is subdivided into production communities and reports the presence of many *klalas* whose members may belong to different lineages. At least some of these *klalas* come into being through the temporary and occasional fusion of several *klalas* into pairs (pp. 182–83).

In its different forms the *klala*—whether it be in pairs or extended—appears to be a substitute institution which develops where the bonds of lineage have been weakened. This usually happens for historical reasons—secessions, migrations, or the effects of trade and war:

> This institution [the *klala*—E.T.] seems to be fairly widespread among the Guro. It is certainly known by the same

name in many villages and is most often found where the lineage structure is weakest. (p. 181)

The *klala* group is sometimes composed of landless youths who work for their elders: in that case it is a direct substitute for lineage cooperation. Sometimes it is manned by adults who already hold one or more plots of land and cultivate them in succession. In this case its egalitarian structure is its distinguishing mark, differentiating it from lineage cooperation: the *klala* group is run on the basis of strict reciprocity and does not appear to have its own leader or institutionally recognized organizer. When the *klala* takes the place of lineage cooperation the distribution of the product—the *klala* has neither gifts nor feasts—and the appropriation of the means of production continue to be performed within the framework of the lineage. In this sense the *klala* remains subordinate to the lineage structure. In the forests, where traditional society has been preserved free from outside interference, it appears that the relations of production corresponding to simple cooperation are "realized" in what can be described as the *lineage system*.

It has been shown that simple cooperation has two sub-forms, restricted and extended cooperation. Which of these is dominant? This will be determined by a study of the allocation of the means of production and the distribution of the product. Here two types of means of production are brought into play, tools and land. Wooden tools, mortars, pestles, canoes,

> though they are made to meet the demands of an individual, are not his exclusive property. They can better be described as goods for collective use which are very freely borrowed and lent. (p. 191)

As for iron tools, Meillassoux has the following to say:

Iron tools are in general use. Unlike the objects mentioned before, however, they are not goods for collective use but are the exclusive property of the elders. Thus the number of machetes owned by the leader of the community is equal to that of the men working under his authority, while the number of hoes corresponds to the number of women. (p. 193)

It can be seen that the instruments of labor may be at the disposal of the individual or the work-team, but are in neither case their property. The same applies to land. Each plot is subject to a series of superimposed rights: the right of the tribe in relation to other tribes, that of the village in relation to other villages, that of the lineage in relation to other lineages in the village. These rights, however, are of a negative nature: they exclude foreign communities from using the plots. In fact, they are the juridico-political "reflection" of the allocation of the land as a means of production. Positive rights are found only at the level of the lineage, in the actual allocation: it is at this level that plots are allocated and agricultural work is organized. The real ownership of land is vested in the lineage in the person of its elder:

Whenever the huntsmen came upon land suitable for cultivation, they demarcated it by blazing trees and informed the elder of their community. He, in turn, arranged for this reserved land to be worked by dividing the labor involved among those under his jurisdiction . . . , the right to cultivate a separate field being a function of the social rank held by each of them. (p. 259)

In short, the lineage is the "realization" of the *production community* which corresponds to extended cooperation, and is the "locus" from which the allocation of the principal means of production is carried out.

An analysis of the relations of distribution confirms this interpretation. The unit of consumption for foodstuffs is not identical with the *work-team* based on restricted cooperation, but with the *production community* based on extended cooperation:

> [The harvest] is stored in community granaries under the direct or indirect control of the elder. The second brother or first wife is often the manager. The primary use for the produce is the feeding of the community, sometimes a temporary guest, a few relatives from a neighboring village, or the members of a *bo*. Usually only a small proportion is sold or exchanged. The doyen of the community is the axis around whom the circulation of the goods revolves. The produce of the group goes to him, and then most if not all of it returns to the members of the community. (p. 188)

The principal daily meal is taken in the evening and theoretically all members of the *dogi* participate. A further division then takes place into groups based on age and sex which are not co-terminous with the work-teams.

> This rather confused mechanism serves to redistribute foodstuffs to all members of the community and thus the collective meal can be seen as the end result of the process of agricultural cooperation: the unspecified labor of each is returned in a common product. All have mixed their labor and all participate in the use of the product of the labor of all the others. (pp. 124–25)

Distribution follows the same pattern in the areas in which hunting predominates. The precious products of trapping and gathering are entrusted to the elder:

> Tusks acquired by hunting, trapping, or finding dead elephants belong to the hunter, that is, to the man who initiated and directed the expedition. When the hunter, as is usual, is under the jurisdiction of an elder, the tusks go to

him. It is usually the hunters who come upon groves of kola palms during their trips. The beneficiary of the discovery is the elder of the discoverer. The entire produce picked by the women and children of the community goes to him. (p. 189)

The same applies to handicrafts:

The artisan is always integrated into a social unit built around agricultural activities. . . . Consequently, the product of his labor will usually circulate within his community following the pattern described above: objects are made for the benefit of the doyen or the community as a whole and the only return the artisan receives for his labor is the food he shares with those in his meal group, in exactly the same way as if he had been participating in agricultural work. (pp. 189–90)

We shall further examine the exact part played by the elder in the appropriation of the means of production and the distribution of the product. What concerns us here is the fact that in both cases the elder enjoys a privileged position as the representative of the lineage. Recapitulating, it is clear that the lineage "realizes" the production community based on extended cooperation, while the segment of a lineage or extended family "realizes" the work-team based on restricted cooperation. An examination of the relations of property and distribution shows clearly that, in the social relations of production corresponding to simple cooperation, the production community prevails over the work-team, and extended cooperation over restricted cooperation.

Finally, it is necessary to describe the structures of control the supervision involved in these relations of production, that is, to embark upon an analysis of the institution of the "elder." This is a two-fold question: first, we must define the role of the elder and second, we must seek the reason why this role is usually performed by old men.

With regard to the first point, we have seen that the production community is divided into work-teams. Thus there is a two-fold appropriation of the means of production: *ownership* is vested in the production community, but the work-team enjoys their *use*. The production community must divide the means of production between its component work-teams, and this implies that it embraces the position or function of one who *carries out the division*. The social persona of the elder is defined by the fact that he occupies this position and performs this task. It follows that the elder is often also the organizer of cooperation, though the existence of the *klala* shows that this is not always the case. Why are the "elders" recruited from the ranks of mature or old men? As Meillassoux himself has suggested (p. 188), the answer can be found in his article on traditional self-subsistence economies, published after the book on the Guro.[14] This article came after the author's field work and was certainly inspired by it. He shows that in segmentary societies, where the productive force of labor is poorly developed, the authority of the elders cannot be directly based on any of the following:

—Physical constraint, because the elders are the weakest members of the community, both physically and numerically.

—Kinship in the biological sense, because the only form of domination kinship as such can create is that of parents over young children.

—Control of the land, both because it is abundant, and because the elders need the young to protect the groups' land against strangers and have no force which could resist the demands of the young on this land.

—Finally, control of the instruments of production, because tools are individual and are made of material accessible to all, or of rare or imported material on which the elders hold a monopoly by virtue of their privileged position (but in the latter case, the privilege explains the monopoly and not vice versa).

To put it another way, the control of physical force, the prerogatives attached to social paternity, control over land, and the instruments of production, can all become the attributes of authority but cannot be its source or foundation. These attributes can be acquired from a position of authority, but they cannot explain why the position exists or why it is occupied by particular persons. Various elements combine to form the overall conditions of production and only one of these appears to come under the immediate and, in a sense, "natural" control of the elders: this is knowledge, the sum of technical know-how necessary for production. Meillassoux puts this very well:

> The acquisition of technical knowledge gives its possessor real authority over the ignorant since the perpetuation of the group depends upon it. . . . New knowledge is acquired over time and increases with physiological age—not necessarily in an absolute sense, but in a sufficiently regular fashion to justify the basic relationship of elder and youth. Thus the acquisition and preservation of knowledge tends to reinforce the authority of older persons over those younger.[15]

The authority of the elders in the area of production can only be understood as resulting from their appropriation of knowledge. However, the nature of the source also explains the narrow limits of the authority. In fact,

> in this kind of society the sum of essential technical knowledge is limited, and can be acquired in a relatively short time. It tends to put all men above a certain age on an equal footing.[16]

Meillassoux shows that in some societies the elders try to create artificial reinforcements for their control over knowledge by extending it beyond the essentials or putting up institutional barriers to its acquisition—for instance, initiation rites. However, there seem to be no such barriers among the Guro. In my view such procedures can, in any case, only consolidate the power they owe to this control and not extend it. As for what can be called "social knowledge," this does not play a direct part in production but in the reproduction of the social structure, and it is in a study of reproduction that its effects become apparent. In brief, the relative simplicity of technical knowledge makes it a minor element in the overall conditions of production. The appropriation of such a minor element can only give the elders limited power over the process of production as a whole.

With regard to the area of relations of political authority, it now seems clear that the power of the elder is essentially a functional power. The authority of the elder certainly weighs heavily on the unmarried young men and on those whose marriages are as yet childless, but it grows less effective as the youth grows older and establishes his own authority over his own descendants and dependents. There are several stages in this process of emancipation: the younger man is first given the responsibility of a work-team, then of a plot of land, and finally part of the product is put entirely at his disposal. Passage from stage to stage is dependent upon the increasing social status of the younger man, which is not solely dependent upon the goodwill of the elder. The latter can, certainly, delay the time for handing over land and women, and thus slow down the process of emancipation, but it would be difficult for him to block it completely as the youth would then have several courses open to him:

Social promotion often involves conflict between the elder and his junior. In such cases the elders of the village are called upon to arbitrate.

It is obvious that the elders have mutual interests and the *wiblizà* [members of the council of elders] in fact almost always support their peers. The dependent junior then has no recourse but to submit, to go into exile, or to confront his elder with a *fait accompli* by refusing to partake of the collective meal (always a sign of discord), and by cultivating his own land while refusing to work on that of the community. The youth would only take such grave steps if he were sure of support, which he would usually seek from his maternal family. (p. 171)

As an example Meillassoux cites a quarrel between Tro and his son Tiese which ended in the capitulation of Tro:

For a year Tiese refused to work for his father, setting himself up in a bush encampment and clearing a plot of lineage ground for himself. Tro was loath to try to stop this for fear that Tiese would take refuge with his maternal family. It is said that in the end, after a year of this, Tro forgave his son. (p. 171)

The same applies to the distribution of foodstuffs: the elder is guardian of the community's reserves, and these are distributed under his authority. But, to return to the text quoted above,

The product of the group goes to the elder, but most, if not all, of it returns to the members of the community. (p. 188)

Up to this point in the investigation it appears that it would be very difficult for the elders to transform their functional authority into the power to exploit. It remains to be seen whether their role in the reproduction of the total social structure, especially in the allocation of women, provides any better opportunity to achieve such a purpose.

Rules Governing Animal Husbandry

The means of production brought into play in animal husbandry are the land and the livestock put out to pasture. Grazing land is the collective property of the villagers in the sense that it is left undivided and available to all who own stock. On the other hand, the livestock is the individual property of the elders and the wealthy. A study of the relations of distribution shows, however, that the individual ownership of livestock does not lead to a form of private property in the modern sense of the term. It is, in fact, the lineage which holds the herd through the elder, who cannot use it except for communal purposes:

> The Guro did not consume the milk from their animals, which were not bred strictly as a source of food. They were only occasionally slaughtered simply for meat and then only by the richest men with many cattle. It was more usual for cattle to be ritually sacrificed in propitiatory or expiatory ceremonies, as and when recommended by the diviners. The meat was then eaten communally or divided between the members of the village or even those of the whole tribe, according to the size of the ceremony. . . . Hoofed animals were also exchanged in marriage settlements, and used as compensation or fines for serious offenses. (p. 103)

This shows that the ownership of grazing land is subject to the same rules as the ownership of arable land: just as anyone can freely take out of the village reserve of land such plots as he wishes to bring under cultivation (pp. 259–60), so any stock-owner can put his beasts onto the communally owned pasture. Livestock as a product is governed by the same rules as surplus food: the elder controls it but cannot use it for his own private purposes. Thus it appears that the production process in agriculture and in animal husbandry proceeds within the same framework of relations of production. We should note, however, one institution which appears to be connected only with animal husbandry: this is a system of patronage whereby elders and notables possessing livestock extend their social relations and influence beyond the limits of their own village:

> It is possible that embryonic relations of patronage were formerly built around livestock. These could have been based on the practice of guardianship (*drivâva*) . . . It was customary to entrust an inhabitant of a strange village with the care of one's cows as a favor. Only female animals were so entrusted: the first, second, and fourth offspring or litter remained the property of the owner, the guardian kept the third and fifth, and then the original animal was returned. (p. 104)

Should this institution be considered an indication of an autonomous system of relations of production? Because of their mobility, livestock can be lent out and thus provide the basis for a system of patronage. No elder can grant a plot of land to anyone strange to the village without the collective agreement of the villagers because land is both cultivatable field and hunting ground. The elder can dispose of it in its first aspect, but not its second, where the village remains collectively sovereign. Since it is impossible to dissociate these two aspects, land cannot be lent. Obviously no such restriction applies to livestock. Do these special instances suffice to make patronage a specific relation of production? I think not: when an elder lends livestock to a stranger he makes the latter his junior; to become a patron is to extend the lineage beyond its genealogical limits. In this connection it is significant that the patronage relationship is expressed in kinship terms:

> Kinship is a social category and therefore relations of protection, of production, of patronage, or of enslavement set

up with a stranger will be defined in terms of a kinship relationship corresponding to the position occupied by the
adopted person in the hierarchy of the group. (p. 65)

How then do the regulations governing animal husbandry relate to those governing agriculture? In their most
significant aspects the system of productive forces governing the two branches is the same: the principle means of
production—in the one case land, in the other land and
livestock—are both object and means of labor. Restricted
cooperation applies to animal husbandry in the same way
it does to agriculture. Finally, the two labor processes are
carried out almost entirely within the same relations of
production. The special feature described in animal husbandry—patronage—is due to the adaptation of the relations of production "realized" in the lineage system to the
material characteristics of the means of production, livestock. It does not, however, make any difference to the nature of the relations of production. In effect, agriculture
and animal husbandry in this society are related in the
same way as industry and agriculture under the advanced
capitalist mode of production: the special features of the
latter—the role of the landowner, etc.—are not sufficiently
significant to make the relations of production in agriculture into an autonomous system in relation to the relations of production in industry; in both cases the mode of
production is capitalist. Here too, the relations of production "realized" under the lineage system dominate
both agriculture and animal husbandry. Of course, this situation is not common to all "primitive" socioeconomic
formations. An analysis of Peul, Masai, or Nuer societies
would lead to quite different conclusions.

Captivity

Our study of the social relations of production would be
incomplete if I made no reference to captivity, which

Meillassoux describes as follows:

> The Guro traditionally practiced a form of domestic slav-
> ery which applied to no more than a handful of persons.
> . . . Domestic slaves were subject to the commands of their
> masters or the wives and were used for field work, carrying
> water, building huts, etc. The most skillful and those who
> enjoyed the confidence of their masters undertook more
> important tasks, such as weaving, fishing, or hunting the ele-
> phant on their behalf. Even though they were entirely sub-
> ject to the authority of the master, who had the power of
> life and death over them and could sell them, domestic
> slaves were associated with the kinship system: they shared
> the communal meal, eating it with their masters; they might
> even inherit from them if they had no heirs. They were mar-
> ried according to the exogamous rules of the lineage to
> women of other lineages, usually to other slaves for whom a
> bride-price was paid; but sometimes a higher bride-price was
> paid to marry one to a free woman. The doyen of the com-
> munity adopted the children of slaves and, with the passing
> of the generations, the distinction of rank became blurred
> to vanishing point. (pp. 203–4)

It is clear that the captives were in effect juniors whose
subjection was more complete and whose emancipation
was a longer process. The relations of captivity do not,
therefore, involve an autonomous system, but are integrated into the lineage system which thus has a dual foundation: biological kinship and captivity.

MODES OF PRODUCTION

It is now possible to identify the mode or modes of
production operating in Guro society. It must be remembered that a mode of production comprises both a system
of productive forces and a system of relations of pro-

duction. It is an association of producers and means of production determined by two relations: material appropriation and distribution. If we look at this definition in the light of the analysis carried out above, we can see that the socioeconomic formation of the Guro results from the combination of two modes of production:

—The first, revealed in complex cooperation, is "realized" in what we have called the tribal-village system. In the category of relations of production, ownership of the means of production is collective and the rules of distribution are egalitarian. In the juridico-political category, this mode of production entails the existence of authority functioning intermittently and temporarily, performed in turn by all the men of the group—although, in the long run, the most distinguished acquire a purely moral authority.

—Simple cooperation reveals the presence of the second mode of production, which is "realized" in what we have called the lineage system, or in its substitute, the *klala* system. In the category of relations of production, the means of production are owned collectively but a single individual holds them on behalf of the group. The product is divided according to the mechanism Karl Polanyi has called "redistribution":[17] levies from the periphery going to the center, gifts going from the center to the periphery. Finally, this mode of production entails authority functioning continuously, entrusted to persons selected by virtue of their age.

THE RULES AND FUNCTIONS OF KINSHIP RELATIONS

We have seen that in the socioeconomic formation of Guro society the lineage system "realizes" the relations of

Table 2
The Socioeconomic Structure of the Guro

	First Mode of Production	Second Mode of Production
Factors of production:	First system of factors	Second system of factors
Object of labor	Land	Land, which is also the means of labor
Technical knowledge	Relatively simple	Relatively simple
Implements of production	Collective	Individual

Form of cooperation
 	
Dominant element in this combination:
form of cooperation
	Complex	Simple, comprising a combination of two sub-forms:
		    Extended cooperation
		    Restricted cooperation
		Dominant sub-form:
		    Extended cooperation

Production unit	The village and the hunting groups (*seriwue, be'i,* and *bebu*)	—The production community which corresponds to extended cooperation —The work-team which corresponds to restricted cooperation *The community predominates over the work-team*
Overall relations of production	Tribal-village system	The lineage system or its substitute, the *klala*
Ownership of the means of production	Collective	Vested in the elder as a representative of the productive community
Distribution of the product	Egalitarian sharing	Redistributed by the elder
Authority relations	Periodic, temporary functional authority: vested in persons recruited according to merit	Continuous, functional authority: vested in persons recruited according to age
Note: Branches where these modes of production operate	Hunting with nets	Agriculture, fishing, gathering, hut-building, trapping of large animals Animal husbandry

production and the superstructural relations associated with simple cooperation. The production units correspond to the latter, work-teams and production communities take the form of extended families and segments of lineages or entire lineages—that is, of kinship groups. In the same way, the relation between elder and junior links related persons: a "father" and his "children," a "big brother" and his "little brothers." Thus the lineage system appears as a determined totality of kinship relations. We are thus led to ask ourselves first to try and define the theoretical rules governing these relations, and second, to find an explanation for the importance of their role in the socioeconomic formation of the Guro and in many other "primitive" societies.

The ideology of the structuralists suggests a possible answer. Engels stressed that in the stage of barbarism the mode of production was less important than "the degree in which the old blood bonds and the old mutual community of the sexes within the tribe have been dissolved." [18] Without searching for the cause of this lesser importance, Claude Lévi-Strauss agreed that in primitive societies the rules of kinship and marriage "have an operational value equal to that of economic phenomena in our own society." [19] Hence ethnology should abandon the analysis of the economic infrastructure for that of kinship relations, as only these lead to an account of the "profound structure" of primitive societies. The latter would no longer be the proper preserve of historical materialism, and the autonomy of social anthropology would be justified by the irreducible specificity of its subject. Economic activities, as well as many other activities, would be carried on within the fixed framework of kinship relations.

This is not the place for a critique of this concept, but it must be noted that kinship relations do not dominate the overall social organization of all primitive socioeconomic formations; such domination is associated with the presence of particular modes of production. In the Guro socioeconomic formation two modes of production were observed, one corresponding to complex cooperation and the other to simple cooperation: only in the second does kinship play a special role. Other modes of production, or the same in a different combination, are "realized" in other socioeconomic formations: in these cases kinship relations do not play a dominant role. For example, the economy of the Mbuti pygmies is based on food-gathering and on collective hunting with bows and arrows or nets, carried out very much as they are among the Guro. In commenting on Colin Turnbull's material on the Mbuti, Meillassoux notes that:

> The kinship system is very elementary. . . . The nuclear family is quite weak as a social unit. . . . Genealogical memory does not cover more than two generations. . . . Thus kinship does not constitute a durable bond or form the basis of the social organization.[20]

Masai society could be analyzed along the same lines: the principal activity is animal husbandry and the organization is based on the concept of age sets.

To conclude, it is unwise to assume an automatic association between the predominance of kinship relations and that of agriculture: the data from the Guro have shown that the social framework for agricultural production could be provided by the various forms of *klala* as well as by the lineage system. In none of these cases could an analysis of kinship reveal the fundamental structure of the whole society. In a more general way, the process of making kinship into a single theoretical entity seems to me

no better than the invention of "totemism," so justly condemned by Claude Lévi-Strauss: it brings together under
one heading systems whose position and functions are not
the same in every socioeconomic formation. Some of these
systems organize social life as a whole, while others affect
only some sectors, and these again differ widely: in some
cases it may be production, in others consumption, or in
still others, marriage contracts. To give kinship studies a
strategically decisive value for the understanding of primitive societies, "kinship" must be understood as more than
a simple combination of terms and attitudes, and kinship
systems must be considered in their functional aspect as
much as in their formal aspect: at this point the unity of
the entity "kinship" can no longer be thought of as given
and has to be proved.

Meillassoux's data point in a very different direction.
Concerned to keep the economic base as the determinant
phase of the overall structure, he gives a brilliant demon-
stration of the way in which the lineage system in the
Guro socioeconomic formation derives from a transformation of genealogical kinship relations, a transformation determined and shaped by the requirements of production:

> The agricultural community is modeled on the lineage or
> segment of a lineage. Relations of production are built on
> the basis of genealogical kinship relations, which are them-
> selves subject to constant modification and renewal. The
> kinship relations revealed to us are the result of these
> changes. . . . Life and death act as disturbances and tend to
> break down the natural family. Economic imperatives,
> among others, contribute to the creation of new units
> whose members are tied by relations of production and con-
> sumption. The biological family cannot stay within its nar-
> row genealogical framework and is replaced by functional
> families whose members are associated by economic obliga-

tions rather than by relationships of consanguinity. Under such a dynamic, the bonds of kinship have to be sufficiently elastic to adapt to such modifications; classificatory kinship terms foreshadow the relationship which may be established between individuals in the event of the death of the relative who is the link between them. (pp. 168–69)

The difficult problem of the interplay between kinship relations and relations of production is illuminated by this crucial text. Meillassoux states that the cycle of birth and death ceaselessly destroys and rebuilds "natural" families, but these natural families are constantly reorganized and manipulated into effective production units. Thus kinship relations have a "genealogical" base, but this base is first modified to meet the requirements of production so that relations of production can be "realized" within it. The modification is carried out by a process of selection in the course of which certain genealogical relations are retained and recognized as social relations, while others are "forgotten" or socially assimilated into the former. By the same process the genealogical base thus adapted can again be modified should the need arise for it to cover juridico-political and ideological relations (which will depend on the absence or presence of such factors as the social division of labor, the separation of town and country, class antagonisms, the state—in the last analysis, of the level of development of the economic base). The juridico-political and ideological phases also have specific requirements which do not necessarily accord with those of production or with the genealogical foundation of the overall structure. In segmentary societies, where the lineage structure "conducts" some or all of the social relations, the "real" kinship relations observed by the ethnologists are the result of a compromise between these different groups of requirements.

By pursuing this line of thought Meillassoux avoids two symmetrical temptations which have seduced all too many Marxist investigators. The first sees kinship relations as in some way *created* or *generated* by relations of production; the second visualizes them as arising independently, after which certain economic, juridical, political, or religious functions are attributed or *added* to them from *outside*, but are performed without in any way modifying the kinship relations as such. It would, for example, be absurd to *deduce* the kinship system of Murngin society from its economic base alone. On the other hand, it is inadequate to say that kinship relations "function as relations of production, in the same way as political, religious, etc., relations function" and that "kinship is thus both infrastructure and superstructure." [21] To stop at this is simply to apply new terms to that functional polyvalence of "primitive" institutions which has long been known to classical anthropology, and in fact to thus adopt the structuralist position. If kinship relations are to be explained, the "material" of which they are composed must first be identified. Meillassoux's use of the term "genealogical base" gives only a pointer in that direction. Once the "material" is identified, it is then necessary to show how the economic, juridico-political, and ideological phases *transform* it and make it possible for it to take on the various functions incumbent upon it within the framework of the level of development of the economic base. In other words, concrete kinship relations must be seen as the *product* of a threefold causality operating upon a given substratum, as the combined *effect* upon it of the action of the three phases of the mode of production.

It follows from this analysis that "kinship" should not be seen as a specific phase characteristic of modes of production "realized" in "primitive" socioeconomic formations. These structures exhibit the same system of phases as are found in the modes of production of slavery, feudalism, and capitalism studied by Marx. What then is the correct theoretical status of kinship in these structures? It is a typical case of "super-determination," as Louis Althusser uses the term:

> Super-determination is used to designate . . . the conjunction of different determinations in a single object, and the variations in dominance between the determinations within their very conjunction.[22]

Althusser takes the example of social classes to illustrate this concept:

> To conceive of the nature of a social class it is essential to bring together the determinations of the economic base, of the juridico-political superstructure, and of the ideological superstructure. It is equally essential to be aware of the interplay within this combined determination so as to account for the way in which dominance may shift between the different determinations. . . . [Social classes] are super-determined because their nature can only be understood by invoking the structural causality of the three levels in the society, economic, political, and ideological. This structural causality takes the form of a conjunction of the three structural determinations in a single object, and in the variation of the dominant element within this conjunction.[23]

This text, in my opinion, applies word for word to kinship relations, which thus appear as the structural equivalent, in "primitive" socioeconomic formations, of class relations in socioeconomic formations dominated by slavery, feudalism, or capitalism. But understand: I am not saying here that kinship relations are class relations, that kinship relations show the antagonisms characteristic of class relations, etc. I am saying that both are the complex result of the interplay of the economic, juridico-political, and ideological phases of the mode of production. It follows that the analysis of kinship relations should deal with its subject in the same way the analysis of class relations deals with its. It should distinguish:

—An economic aspect or level in which all the following are "realized": the division of the labor force, that is, the division of the community into kinship groups of varying ranks (for instance, lineages, segments, and extended families in uni-linear groups) corresponding to varying types of production units; the division of the means of production between these units; the organization of consumption units; the structures of direction and control which ensure the coordination and continuity of production.

—A juridico-political aspect or level in which the following are "realized": the determination of the personal status of individuals; the regulations governing property and inheritance; relations of authority and their effects on the formation of those organizations (assemblies of adults, councils of elders) which ensure the smooth running of social life in general.

—An ideological aspect or level in which the ideological conditions for the functioning of the system are "realized": for instance, the kinship system of the Dida, which seems very close to that of the Guro, is associated with an ideology which affirms the principle of solidarity among "brothers," emphasizes the primacy of age allied to wisdom, and regards conflicts between relatives as "monstrous" and usually due to the operation of sorcery.[24]

When this parallel between class relations and kinship relations has been drawn one essential problem remains, posed by the existence in kinship relations of a genealogical base acted upon by the three phases of the mode of production. No attempt will be made here to define the nature of this base, since the necessary theoretical tools are not yet available. On the other hand, it is possible to inquire into the conditions of its operation: in fact, this calls for a distinction between two different ways in which a mode of production can be realized in a socioeconomic formation. Certainly, both class relations and kinship relations are the result of the interplay of the phases of the mode of production. However, while an analysis of this interplay is sufficient to account for class relations, an unexplained residual element remains where kinship relations are concerned. In socioeconomic formations dominated by the capitalist mode of production, the action of the phases *alone* produces class relations; here kinship relations are the effect of the action of the phases on a material, or rather on an *element*, which cannot be reduced to this action. Thus the mode of production is *directly* realized in one socioeconomic formation and *indirectly* in the other. It is obvious that the reasons for this difference must be sought in the structure of the modes of production concerned. We here present some hypotheses which may contribute to the solution of this problem.

The first question we must ask ourselves is the exact extent of the difference observed between direct and indirect realization: is direct realization the rule or the exception? An examination of socioeconomic formations with a class structure permits us to make a preliminary observation. We know that Marx considered that classes did not appear in a "pure form" until the capitalist mode of production had established its hegemony. When any other mode of production—for instance, slave-based or feudal— is predominant, classes appear in the form of castes, orders, or estates. It is very tempting to see here the opposition referred to above: in one case the classes may be realized directly, in the other they will be realized in an "element" whose nature remains to be defined. Of course, extensive research would be required to verify such a proposition. But if we accept it provisionally, the problem becomes more precise: in fact, direct realization appears to be a trait characteristic of socioeconomic formations dominated by the capitalist mode of production and must, therefore, be explained by reference to the other features peculiar to this mode of production.

If it is correct that classes appear in a pure form only in socioeconomic formations dominated by the capitalist mode of production, this appears to me to be because the economic base in this mode of production is not only *determinant*, as it is in other modes of production—it not only defines the part played by each phase in the production of concrete social formations, it is also *dominant* and itself plays the principal part in this production. Mercantile production becomes capitalist when labor itself becomes merchandise. At this point mercantile relations cease to govern only the circulation of products between units of production; they penetrate into these units. The ability of the capitalist to set up a production unit under his management is derived from the purchase of labor from the workers; it is by selling his labor to the capitalist that the worker can, on the one hand, gain access to the means of production and become a producer and, on the other hand, obtain the means of subsistence for himself and his family. This transaction between capitalists and workers conditions the very existence of the production unit, for it is the only means of bringing together the various factors which interact to form the labor process.

When mercantile relations come to dominate the sphere of production as completely as that of circulation, they become the fundamental social bond:

It is the basic precondition of bourgeois society that labor directly produces exchange value, therefore, money; and that money then directly buys labor, which the worker hence sells only insofar as he himself offers his activity in exchange. Wage labor on the one hand, capital on the other, are thus simply other forms of developed exchange value and of money as its embodiment. It follows that money is directly both the reality of the community insofar as it is the substance of existence for all individuals, and is also their common product.[25]

This relationship excludes all others. In the feudal mode of production, relations of personal dependence united the producer to the owner of the means of production, but the disappearance of such relations was a precondition for the establishment of the hegemony of the capitalist mode of production in which worker and capitalist confront each other solely as buyer and seller in the labor market. Outside this market they are strangers indifferent to each other: "[Avarice] itself is the essence of the community and can permit nothing to take precedence over it." [26]

It is now clear why classes only appear in a pure form in socioeconomic formations dominated by the capitalist mode of production. A class is defined by the function of its members in social production. However, it is only when the economic phase dominates the mode of production that this function can become the immediate principle of production of concrete social groups; as long as the relations of production are not exclusively economic this function cannot by itself account for the identity of social groups, nor serve directly as the basis for differentiating them.

The advent of capitalist production is conditional upon the divorce of the laborer from the means of production on the one hand, and the existence of the free laborer on the other. What were characteristic of pre-capitalist modes of production, on the contrary, were *non-economic* bonds between producers, means of production, and sometimes also non-producers. These bonds were not only the political or ideological representation of the relations of production, but also entered into them as constituent elements. This presence clearly shows us that in these modes of production the political and ideological superstructure was dominant. In primitive socioeconomic formations as described by Marx, the unity between labor and its material conditions is mediated by the laborers' membership in a commune, and the individual's access to the means of production is through this commune; in the slave-based mode of production the violence of the master relegates the slave to the position of one among several means of production and makes possible the process of production based on slavery. In the feudal mode of production the production process is both a process of appropriation of nature and one of exploitation of labor, and this requires the existence of a relation of personal dependence between the direct producers and the owners of the land. In both cases, whatever their nature and the violence of the antagonisms underlying them, these are non-economic bonds uniting the members of the production unit and bringing them into contact with the means of production. Thus in pre-capitalist modes of production these bonds perform the functions belonging to mercantile relations in the capitalist mode of production.

This alternative function reflects a vast difference in the structures of the modes of production concerned. It is not sufficient to describe this difference by stating that in one case the economic base is dominant and in the other the ideological and political superstructures are dominant.

The domination of the economic base really implies its *relative autonomy* with regard to the superstructures, which become simply the representation of the relations of production laid down outside their scope. The dominance of the superstructures, on the other hand, implies the *relative integration* of the three phases of the mode of production: it appears when a juridical, political, or ideological link becomes a condition of the process of production and the superstructures are consequently and by necessity introduced into the economic base itself.

This seems to justify the view that an effect and a sign of this difference in the structure of the mode of production can be found in the absence or presence in the process of realization of an "element" acted upon by the three phases and so transformed as to produce concrete social relations: I think it is the relative integration of the phases within the mode of production which leads to the convergence of their determinations onto one single element. Economic, juridico-political, and ideological sectors can be clearly distinguished in socioeconomic formations dominated by the capitalist mode of production because of the relative autonomy of its phases: each phase has a sort of area of realization which is reserved to it. Consequently the analysis can begin by allocating to each of the sectors the concrete social formations described by the historian or the sociologist; super-determination will be produced on the basis of such an allocation. When pre-capitalist modes of production are dominant such an allocation is only possible in the course of the investigation. In such modes of production juridico-political and ideological phases are involved in the very economic base of the mode of production: this involvement invalidates the delineation within the socioeconomic formation of distinct sectors corresponding to each of the phases. The three phases are inseparably involved in the mode of production and have a common area of realization, here called an "element." It follows that it would be wrong at this point to allocate concrete social forms produced in these conditions to one phase or another: a lineage often appears to be a production unit, a political body, and a sort of religious "congregation"; only after close examination of these various determinations and their combinations can it be decided which of them is the dominant determination. This brings us back to the functional polyvalence of institutions that I described earlier, and which I have simply wished to show was the result of a specific structure of the mode of production.

This discussion has been focused on identifying the necessary condition for an "element" to play a part in the realization of any mode of production: this condition has proved to be the domination of the mode of production concerned by one of the phases of the superstructure. We must now return to the search for the necessary conditions for kinship to act as such an element. Here again the theory of the capitalist mode of production can serve as a guideline. To recapitulate, the specific characteristic of this mode of production is the transformation of the labor force into merchandise and the introduction of mercantile relations into the very heart of the immediate production process. This introduction has the necessary effect of divorcing production from individual consumption or, to be more precise, dissociating the production unit from the consumption unit. This dissociation is expressed in two ways. First, the production and consumption units—or, as contemporary economics would call them, the enterprise and the household—become social units quite different from each other in both size and structure. Second, the only bonds that remain between them are those of trade:

when the product leaves the production process it must necessarily pass through the market before being available for consumption. This raises the question as to whether, inversely, pre-capitalist modes of production were not marked by a tendency to unity of production and consumption, a unity which might vary in degree and take on different forms. The concept of self-subsistence, used by many ethnologists to define "primitive" economies, is obviously a case in point. This is a very equivocal concept, since it really describes three phenomena which can, within certain limits, vary independently of each other. Self-subsistence may be understood as:

1. Where circulation—that is, the link between the production unit and the consumption unit—is non-mercantile.

2. Where production and consumption units are homologous, that is, the two units are constituted on the same principle and by the same mechanism so that they are of the same size and structure.

3. Where production and consumption units are co-terminous, that is, the production unit finds within itself the conditions for its reproduction—raw materials, instruments of production, and stock for consumption.

We have seen that as mercantile relations become the general rule, the production unit is divorced from the consumption unit. In other words, this divorce makes it impossible for production and consumption units to be homologous, let alone co-terminous. But this negative correlation does not have a positive equivalent. It is possible to postulate a system in which the production and consumption units are homologous and circulation is mercantile: this occurs in what is called small-scale family agriculture where the peasant and his family constitute both production unit and consumption unit; they dispose of their produce through the market and find there what they need for their subsistence. Conversely, it is possible to postulate a system in which production and consumption units are not homologous and yet circulation is not mercantile: this happens when labor is communal but consumption remains attached to the family, the product being allocated by redistribution or sharing. Finally, if the production and consumption units are strictly co-terminous any form of mercantile circulation is, of course, ruled out; on the other hand, in a formal analysis this implies that production and consumption units are homologous—since only similar entities can be superimposed—but that they are not to be completely identified: in the Trobriand system of the *urigubu,* for instance, the producer hands most of his produce to the husband of his sister, and receives the bulk of what he consumes from the brother of his wife; in such a case the production and consumption units are certainly homologous but not co-terminus. It is safe to say that, on the one hand, a situation where consumption and production units are perfectly co-terminous—that is to say, autarchy—never occurs and, on the other hand, that when they are homologous this is usually based upon their being partially co-terminous.

If the term self-subsistence is kept for modes of production in which circulation is basically non-mercantile and production and consumption units are homologous, it may be possible to correlate self-subsistence so defined with the presence of "kinship" as an element in the realization of the mode of production. Of course, if a mode of production involves the existence of several kinds of production units, self-subsistence can be identified as long as the consumption unit is homologous with one of these production units, which will be seen to be dominant. This correlation can be illustrated by returning to the Guro. In

the mode of production associated with simple cooperation, the principal production unit—the production community—and the consumption unit—the meal group—are
homologous. Both units comprise the same persons and
are similarly organized; both production community and
meal group bring men and women together. We have seen
that the most important production processes are mixed
and/or alternate, in other words, men and women take
part together or in succession; however, the division of
labor between the sexes "corresponds" to their separation
into distinct sub-groups during the collective meal. In the
same way, the elder exercises direction and control in
production; and during the meal he eats alone or a special
dish is reserved for him. Thus the consumption unit reproduces the structure of the production unit by the "means"
appropriate to it. Similarly, both are "realized" in kinship
relations. The situation is quite different in the mode of
production associated with complex cooperation. Although the consumption unit is still the meal group just
described, the production unit not only comprises all men
of the village and is a far bigger collective unit than the
meal group, but it excludes the women: they cannot,
therefore, be said to be homologous. This involves the
tribal-village system. On the other hand, in the savannah
region, where pre-colonial trade was quite extensive, the
klala has partly replaced the lineage system; in the forest
area, the lineage system is comparatively unchanged. It
can be seen that kinship does not act, or does so less than
formerly, as an element in the realization of the mode of
production in the absence of one of the two characteristics
by which we have defined self-subsistence—homologous
production and consumption units, and underdeveloped
mercantile relations. Conversely, we can see that self-sub-

sistence is a necessary condition for kinship to act in this way.

Insofar as the homologous relationship between production and consumption unit is based on their being partially co-terminous, self-subsistence must involve the presence of *communities* which are both production and consumption units. It is these communities which are organized by kinship relations. Two different possibilities present themselves. In one case, the socioeconomic formation is an aggregate of communities linked by various relations of an economic order (circulation of the labor force, of the means of production, and of the product), or of a political order (war, alliances, etc.). In this case the structure of the community represents that of the socioeconomic formation, and the relations of production which form the basis of the latter are the internal relations of the former and are thus "realized" in kinship relations. In the other case, the socioeconomic formation is composed of communities exploited by a class of non-producers; its structure is no longer represented by that of the community; the relations which form its base are no longer the internal relations of the community, but are instead juridical, political, and ideological relations of dependence which subordinate the community to its exploiters. In fact, the combination of producers and non-producers is not a community in the sense defined earlier. Self-subsistence does not simply disappear when exploitation appears, but it does begin to dissociate the production units from the consumption units; the introduction of consumption by non-producers leads to the growth of consumption units which do not correspond to any production unit. At this point self-subsistence can no longer be considered a characteristic trait of the mode of production, which can no longer be realized in kinship relations. It is true that the direct producers still belong to communities organized by kinship relations; on the other hand, kinship relations can realize the juridical, political, and ideological relations which link the non-producers among themselves; thus they can still realize the relations internal to both the two classes concerned, but can no longer realize the relations *between* these two classes—and it is these latter relations which, correctly speaking, constitute the structure of the mode of production.

Thus it appears that the absence of the exploitation of labor is the second necessary condition for kinship to act as an element in the realization of the mode of production. This brings us back by another route to the thesis supported by Morgan and Engels in the first applications of historical materialism to ethnology: the domination of kinship relations in the social organization is incompatible with the exploitation of labor and the existence of class relations. This thesis will recur when we examine the reproduction of the socioeconomic formation of the Guro.

THE STRUCTURE OF THE SOCIOECONOMIC FORMATION AND RELATIONS BETWEEN THE MODES OF PRODUCTION

What relations link the two modes of production we have identified within the socioeconomic formation of the Guro?

First, it should be noted that the absence of a real social division of labor means that all Guro adult males are engaged in both modes while the women are restricted to the second. This is an extreme case of a situation found in many other socioeconomic formations: the French worker/peasant of the nineteenth century was involved in both the capitalist mode of production and in individual self-subsistence production; the Ivory Coast farmer of the twentieth century is involved in small-scale mercantile production with his cash crops and in collective self-subsistence production with his food crops.

Such a situation arises when the productive force of labor is at a low stage of development. It has the following effect: the problem of the relations between the combined modes of production is here far more acute than where one or more distinct classes corresponds to each mode, as is the case in other socioeconomic formations. The problem presents itself at the level of relations of production: if two systems of relations of production serve to structure the same community, it is necessary first to find their limits and understand their connection, then to enumerate the internal modifications their co-existence brings about in each, and, finally, to discover which of them is the system and hence the dominant mode of production.

With regard to the division of social labor, Meillassoux reports that hunting and war are "the principal activity of the men" (p. 93), although men also engage in agricultural work. Women divide their time between the latter and domestic activities. Thus it would appear that the greater part of social labor is devoted to agriculture.

In the area of relations of production the tribal-village system and the lineage system are related in various ways, depending upon whether the latter is still intact or in the process of breaking down. In the first case, frequent in the forest regions, there is a kind of adjustment between the two systems which makes the passage from one to the other possible without discontinuity: the tribal-village system can be described in a language proper to the lineage system and the links between villages within a tribe are expressed in genealogical terms. The tribe has a founder whose "sons" founded villages and whose "grandsons" founded lineages. Moreover, the division of the village into hunting groups (*seriwuo*) coincides with its division into lineages (p. 97): in Bazré the two *seriwuo* embrace two lineages (p. 97) and, as we have seen, when the bag is shared every participant in the hunting expedition gets a part. Conversely, the organization into hunting groups "even extends into the social life of the village" (p. 98):

> Among the N'Goi . . . at the funeral of a notable member of a *seriwuo* some of the animals sacrificed by the family of the deceased were given to the other *seriwuo*, where a further sharing was made between the *goniwuo* (lineages). At Zaguietta (Gonan) the sacrificial beasts were not divided between *beï* and *bebu*, but in other ways the social extension of the *seriwuo* was much greater. The doyen of the lineages comprising the *seriwuo* exercised de facto authority. . . . Even more significant, I was told that members of the same *seriwuo* could not intermarry . . . (p. 98)

Thus the two systems are partially congruent. Should it be deduced from this that one is the product of the other? I do not think so: there is nothing to justify an a priori decision that the hunting group derives from a union of several lineages or, inversely, that the lineages were formed by the break up of a hunting group. To judge by the Dida example, it seems possible that both these processes were involved.

In the savannah, on the other hand, the lineage system is too weakened to be capable of conducting all social relations. At this stage a sharp distinction separates it and the tribal-village system. Hunting groups, as we have seen, are recruited without regard to lineage, and at the share-out each hunter keeps his own bag. However, the effect of organization into hunting groups ends when the hunters re-enter the village:

> At Duonefla people explain that in the bush it is *beï* and *bebu;* in the village it is the *goniwuo*. (p. 98)

Thus when the two systems are equal in vitality they interact: the lineage system influences the distribution of the catch, while the tribal-village system operates inside the village; and the languages which express them are adjusted to each other and each can be described in the language of the other.

On the other hand, when the lineage system has been undermined the links that unite it to the tribal-village system are weakened and both systems cease to function outside their own spheres. Meillassoux's findings do not show whether, in the savannah region, relations have been established between the hunting groups and the *klala* which are themselves tending to replace the familial and lineage groups in the area of production. In general, though there may be some overlapping, both systems preserve their specific character and autonomy. Moreover, there is only one kind of consumption unit in the Guro socioeconomic formation, the meal group, linked to the lineage system; this is an indication of the extent to which the latter dominates the society.

We should note here that where the population is not divided between the different branches of production and labor is not seasonal, a single mode of residence can be adapted to satisfy equally the requirements of the two systems of relations of production. In fact, the village appears to result from the common effect of these two systems. Its size is geared to meet the needs of collective hunting: its members must be numerous enough to permit the formation of effective hunting groups. On the other hand, the internal organization of the village is determined by the lineage system: a separate area in the village corresponds to each lineage.

In the political arena, the elders are the source of authority and meet together to form a council of elders (*wiblimo*) in each village. The lineage system imposes relations of authority on the overall socioeconomic formation. However, I have shown that the power of the elders is limited in scope and some aspects of the tribal-village system restrict it still further. A good hunter, a skilled *doplaza* (leader) who can attract and catch many deer in his nets, may ultimately acquire prestige and influence by virtue of his exploits (p. 99). The qualities of a good hunter, however, are the strength, endurance, and skill which are the attributes of youth. Similarly, the leader in war is "usually a young warrior" (p. 67). So to a certain extent, collective hunting and war enable the young to impose some limits on the supremacy of the elders: in these activities younger men acquire at least a moral authority rivaling that of their elders. It should be noted that individual hunting calls for the same qualities and produces similar results, making it easier for the young to secede or emigrate:

> Their art gave the best hunters a means of escape from the governance of their elders. They were undoubtedly the least stable elements in the group. Only a good hunter could risk setting up on new land away from his brothers. (p. 95)

From the limited information given by Meillassoux it seems that in the ideological arena the tribal-village system was dominant over the lineage system:

> Traditionally the place of agriculture in cultural life was less important than that of more exalted, less routine, and more masculine activities such as hunting and war. There is no firstfruits or harvest ceremony, no special cult for agriculture, and only rarely is a chicken sacrificed when new land is cleared. (p. 106)

Where does this analysis, which owes much to the observations and criticisms of Pierre-Philippe Rey,[27] lead? We know how Marx defined the domination of one mode of production over another:

> Under all forms of society there is certain industry which predominates over all the rest and whose condition therefore determines the rank and influence of all the rest.
>
> It is the universal light with which all the other colors are tinged and are modified through its peculiarity. It is a special ether which determines the specific gravity of everything that appears in it. . . .
>
> Among nations whose agriculture is carried on by a settled population . . . where agriculture is the predominant industry, such as in ancient and feudal societies, even the manufacturing industry and its organization, as well as the forms of property which pertain to it, have more or less the characteristic features of the prevailing system of land ownership; [society] is then either entirely dependent upon agriculture, as in the case of ancient Rome, or, as in the middle ages, it imitates in its city relations the forms of organization prevailing in the country. . . .
>
> The reverse is true of bourgeois society. Agriculture comes to be more and more merely a branch of industry and is completely dominated by capital.[28]

What do we have here? In the distribution of social labor the lineage system plays a more vital role than the tribal-village system. In actual production the two systems are distinct and autonomous, but the first imposes its consumption relations on the second; in the political arena, the lineage system outweighs the tribal-village system; in the ideological arena, on the other hand, the reverse is the case. It seems natural to conclude that this is a case of "cross-dominance." The work of Marx has furnished us with other examples of this: remember the case of the

Prussian state, where the economic dominance of the capitalist mode of production went with the political dominance of the feudal mode of production.

But it is not enough to assert the fact of this "cross-dominance"; a relevant theory must now be constructed. At the present time I cannot carry out this task, nor, in a more general way, can we think rigorously about the mechanisms which establish the dominance of one mode of production over another. Some analyses of these mechanisms can be found in the works of Marx, but they concern modes of production which coexist in the framework of mercantile production and which confront each other only in the market. Moreover, the dominance of one mode of production by another—for instance, that of slave-based production over small-scale production—should not be confused with the "expulsion" of one mode of production by another—for example, the feudal mode of production by the capitalist. There is probably reason to distinguish those modes of production with which a particular mode of production can coexist from those which are incompatible with it because of its internal structure. The capitalist and socialist modes of production are required by their very structure to conquer all production and should, therefore, be put in a special category. Pierre-Philippe Rey is doubtless right in suggesting that it is through a tangential approach to an analysis of reproduction that an explanation of the dominance of one mode of production over another may be arrived at—since it is at the point of the reproduction of the material conditions and of the relations of production that the two modes of production can enter into relations with each other. But as far as we are concerned, I do not yet have the tools to achieve this analysis.

THE PROCESS OF REPRODUCTION AND
THE NATURE OF THE RELATIONSHIP BETWEEN
ELDERS AND JUNIORS

I would like, as a conclusion, to look at reproduction from a different point of view. We have seen that in the production process the elders exercise only a moderate influence, "represented" politically by a merely functional power. The question arises as to whether this power is increased by the position of the elders in the process of reproduction.

The process of reproduction includes both the process of immediate production and the process of circulation. During the process of circulation the various factors whose interaction constitutes the short-term production process are divided between and within the units of production. One of these processes of circulation is of special importance. It will be remembered that the nature of the instruments of labor used in the Guro socioeconomic formation is such that labor power is the dominant element in the productive process. Meillassoux writes that:

> Human beings . . . are the sole agents of the economy, the only source of energy, the only means of production and reproduction and are, therefore, the axis of all economic relations. (p. 223)

It follows that the reproduction of the social and economic structure largely depends upon the conditions under which the physical reproduction of the group takes place; thus the circulation of the labor force plays the dominant role among the different processes of circulation which ensure renewal of the production units. Leaving aside captivity, this circulation is generally brought about by matrimonial exchanges which create links between the communities. Among the Guro these exchanges are subject to the law of "general exchange" applied through the system of the bride-price: individual A gives B a wife in exchange for a bride-price which will enable him to obtain a wife of his own. This mechanism ensures the two-fold reproduction, physical and social, of the group:

> These [matrimonial] alliances are not independent of the economy. They are the condition of the perpetuation of the group, in that they give endogamous communities a means of reproduction. Owing to the bride-price system, marriages are equally governed by the mode of production, by circulation, and by accumulation of goods. Wealth, derived from the social organization of the economy, makes marriage possible, and is used by those who have it to perpetuate that very organization. Thus natural reproduction, reproduction of the social structures and of the organization of the economy, are all closely associated in a coherent system. (p. 91)

Meillassoux then tells us:

> Control of the economy and the goods derived from it necessarily rests on the control of the producer and not on appropriation of the means of production, which are rudimentary and almost nonexistent when it comes to tools, and abundant when it comes to land. (p. 90)

Control of the producer is, in turn, based on control of women. In his article in *Cahiers d'Etudes Africaines*, Meillassoux calls the child-bearing woman the "producer of the producer." It follows that the elders can only perpetuate their supremacy if they control the circulation of women and bride-prices, and arrange things so that this process reproduces the social structures which sanction this supremacy.

How do the elders come to hold a monopoly on the goods which make up the bride-price? Some of these goods—loincloths, ivory, cattle—are produced in the framework of the mode of production associated with simple cooperation within the Guro socioeconomic formation. The method of "redistribution" which regulates the distribution of the products created by this mode of production puts them at the disposal of the elders. On the other hand, *sompe*—iron ingots—and guns are imported. The Guro obtain *sompe* from Malinke traders in exchange for baskets of kola nuts: we have seen that the entire kola harvest is handed over to the elders, who are thus alone able to obtain the *sompe*. Guns come from Baoulé country and are exchanged for loincloths and livestock, which are controlled by the elders. Thus the young men are practically excluded from owning matrimonial goods. Finally, a certain "social know-how" is required to make effective use of these goods, a knowledge of genealogy, alliances, etc., and it is the elders who have this. Owing to the nature of these goods, this privilege does not have any impact on the field of production:

> One kind of wealth is composed of objects like gold, ivory, or loincloths, which do not enter into the production process and which are not consumption goods. They do not enter into the subsistence economy, but are treasures, prestige-giving goods, the possession of which marks the rank of the owner. *Bro* (*sompe*) considered as a raw material, guns when used for hunting, slaves as labor power, or consumable goods such as large livestock, can all enter into the production process but are usually accumulated in excess of the real and immediate needs of the subsistence economy. (p. 202) . . . Thus the accumulation of idle stocks of useful goods diverts them from their economic purpose and, by hoarding them, turns them into objects of prestige. (p. 204)

> . . . It is one of the conditions of the perpetuation of the
> social structures that wealth that cannot enter directly into
> the production process has little or no impact on the eco-
> nomic infrastructure. (p. 233)

On the other hand, the elders have sole control of matrimonial goods and are able to control the circulation of
wives and bride-prices, and thus the reproduction of the
society. Meillassoux tells us that they thus gain new power.
We have seen the narrow limits of their supremacy in the
field of production; Meillassoux appears to think that the
dominant position of the elders in the process of the circulation of wives and bride-prices enables them to extend
these limits and to transform a simple functional power
into a real power of command:

> The traditional bride-price always comprises a variety of
> goods which are precisely those said to constitute the
> wealth of the elders. . . . The latter are thus the only ones
> able to enter into matrimonial relations. Their wealth en-
> ables them to marry and to take several wives. The others
> are dependent on them to obtain a wife. Therein lies the
> main source of the authority of the elders. (p. 217)

As far as traditional society is concerned, Meillassoux
does not speak of exploitation of the juniors by the elders.
However—and it is one of the few criticisms I have of his
work—his formulation of this matter is sufficiently ambig-
uous so that others who are bolder go to that length. Thus,
in an otherwise remarkable article entitled "Théorie de
l'histoire des échanges, exemple de l'Ouest-Congolais
(Congo-Brazzaville)," Georges Dupré and Pierre-Philippe
Rey, commenting on Claude Meillassoux's work in their
theoretical introduction, write that "prestige-giving goods
amount to a diversion of the product by the elders, who
make special use of it to reinforce the dependence of the

direct producers." [29] Exploitation does, then, take place in traditional society. Georges Dupré and Pierre-Philippe Rey are naturally led to discover class antagonisms within it:

> We shall speak of class conflict in any society where one particular group controls the circulation of a surplus product in such a way that the circulation of this surplus product ensures the reproduction of relations of dependence between the direct producers and this particular group.[30]

The first thing to be said here is that if class antagonisms exist even in lineage-based and segmentary societies, then they are practically universal: only the bands of hunting and gathering pygmies and Nambikwara would be free of them. But in these circumstances the concept of class loses all its power to discriminate between societies, and describes so many heterogeneous forms of reality that it loses all operational value: as Ariane Deluz and Maurice Godelier observe, it is difficult to put into the same category juniors who are all destined to become elders by the normal operation of the social structure and serfs or proletarians who, even in ancient times, were never to become lords or employers.[31] Moreover, if lineage-based and segmentary societies are to be regarded as class societies, either the correlation between the existence of classes and that of the state established by Marx and Engels must be rejected, or else the institutions which together constitute the state —specialized administration, forces of law and order, taxes, etc.—must be discovered in these societies without recourse to notions of "seed" or "embryo," which are the language of social evolutionism but not of historical materialism.

However, these "epistemological" objections are not the most important. One can speak of exploitation when a group of non-producers appropriates to itself by any means a surplus product *created by the labor* of the direct producers. Now, in the land of the Guro prestige-giving goods and matrimonial goods are not in the main produced by the labor of the juniors. Consider livestock. We have seen that the expenditure of social labor in this branch is very small because the techniques of animal husbandry are very elementary. The part played by labor power consists principally of overseeing, which calls for few persons and little time. Animal husbandry is quite marginal to the sector of the Guro economy dominated by the relations of production "realized" in the lineage system: even if it were conceded that it gives rise to some exploitation of the guardians of the herds by the elders, this exploitation would itself be marginal. The trapping of elephants is an occasional activity requiring relatively few active participants. And with regard to loincloths, Meillassoux writes:

> Both prestige-giving loincloths and those used in external trade, to the extent that they are converted into other prestige-giving goods, remain in the hands of the elders. They are more difficult to make [than everyday loincloths—E.T.] and not all men know the process. Their manufacture is usually a specialty of heads of families or a few experienced weavers working for their elders. (p. 195)

These heads of families and experienced weavers cannot really be classified as juniors; at the least, they are juniors well on the way to emancipation.

As for kola nuts, they are collected and transported not by juniors, but by women and children, and exploitation could only be said to apply to these categories of person. The bulk of the labor of juniors is applied to the production of commonplace goods—foodstuffs, objects of everyday utility—and "most, if not all" (p. 188), of these commonplace goods are distributed back to them. The elder keeps a small portion in his possession to enable him to perform the duties—hospitality, funeral duties, etc.,—incumbent on him as representative of the lineage: this does not mean that a surplus product is appropriated, but rather that there are made available to the elder the means necessary for the exercise of his functional power. In any case, "commonplace goods cannot be exchanged for treasures" (p. 221). It is, therefore, impossible for the elder to exchange the surplus foodstuffs in his charge for prestige-giving goods. In brief, real wealth is not to any great extent levied on the labor of the juniors: if there were exploitation it would, in any case, be very mild.

It is true, as Pierre-Philippe Rey rightly points out, that the agricultural work of the juniors enables the elders to give time to weaving. But if the process of matrimonial exchange proceeds normally, this labor of the juniors will be returned to them in the form of wives. As Meillassoux notes:

> The product of the labor of dependents is taken up by the elder, but is returned to them transformed into a natural means (a wife) for acquiring dependents in their turn. (p. 224)

Of course, ever since Rousseau it has been known that the exploitation of one class by another is often disguised as an exchange: "in exchange" for tribute and enforced tasks, the lord protects his serfs; "in exchange" for his labor power, the capitalist supplies the worker with the subsistence necessary for his maintenance. However, what the junior receives here in exchange for his surplus labor is a wife, that is to say, a way of *freeing himself from the control of the elder*. Exploitation would be present if the elder were in a position to interrupt the process of circulation of wives, or divert it to his advantage, or if he could take over the product of the surplus labor of the juniors without obtaining wives for them. In practice, the control exercised by the elders over this process is strictly limited. Doubtless the elder can punish an intractable junior by delaying the moment when a wife is found; but he cannot altogether refuse to find one lest the junior take refuge with another community, particularly that of his maternal family, which would adopt him. It could be argued in rebuttal that it is evident a priori that the elder, in his role of "maternal uncle," will regain the junior he has lost in his role of "father"; experience disproves this. I could list many instances among the Dida where elders fell from office because of their "greed" or "egoism." It is said that such elders have squandered the matrimonial goods entrusted to them, that is to say, kept them for their own use when they should have used them to marry their juniors. Such elders lose office when their juniors depart. Thus the theoretically absolute authority of the elder is in practice restricted.

When bride-price is paid the cycle of reproduction of the social structure is complete. However, while the general principle of ancestral authority is thus preserved and transmitted, it is at the expense of the progressive diminution of the individual authority of the elder. Each bride-price paid, each marriage performed, loosens their hold over one of their dependents since he has been given the means to achieve independence. Even though each such event loosens the bonds which link the elder directly with his juniors, and even though it is always tempting for him to use his wealth to increase the number of his own wives rather than marry off his dependents, the elder cannot avoid this obligation without the risk of seeing his community wither away or burst apart. The other side of his desire to appropriate wives for his own benefit and so neutralize the junior's means of emancipation is his desire to extend and perpetuate his sphere of authority. (p. 223)

The elder's control of imported matrimonial goods does not strengthen his authority either. In fact, commonplace goods cannot be exchanged for prestige-giving goods in the Guro socioeconomic formation, although such an exchange is possible on the frontiers of the territory: Malinké traders accept foodstuffs in exchange for their *sompe* (p. 270). Thus in a way trade also contributes to limiting the hegemony of the elders:

The existence of a new market, rivaling that covered by the elders, and the possibility of selling agricultural products as well as precious goods, made it possible for men of dependent status or from minor lineages to grow richer in spite of their rank and to escape from traditional authority. Trade, especially in the savannah region, seems to be associated with the crumbling of lineages as well as with the upsetting of traditional relations of superiority and inferiority between lineages. (p. 199) . . . By allowing matrimonial wealth to be obtained outside the conventional norms, trade has opened up opportunities for dependent social units—junior segments or even families of clients or slaves —to escape from the authority of the heads of lineages. (p. 275)

However, this opportunity does not entail revolutionary consequences at the structural level because, "while trade disintegrates existing lineages, it contributes to the recreation of communities which function according to the same norms" (p. 276). In short, as Meillassoux puts it, the effects of trade are "neutralized" by the Guro (p. 221, 277n), and this has two complementary results: while preventing the juniors from completely throwing off the authority of the elders, it also prevents the elders from enhancing it.

To sum up, the elder certainly appropriates a portion of the surplus produced by the juniors, but he uses it mainly to obtain wives for the same juniors and thus gives them the opportunity for emancipation. If he fails to honor this obligation, he will find that his dependents leave him and it will follow that he loses his position as elder. In the same sense, while the consent of the worker is a fictitious condition of the power of the capitalist—the worker can leave one employer but is constrained to sell his labor power to another who will exploit him in the same fashion—so the consent of the junior is a real condition of the power of the elder—because the junior can leave an elder who has not given him a wife for one who will, thus giving him the means to become an elder in his turn. In these circumstances Georges Dupré and Pierre-Philippe Rey are wrong in thinking one can speak of exploitation or class antagonism.*

---

* Of course, it cannot be ruled out a priori that in some circumstances the articulation of trade relations introduced by colonization upon "lineage-type" relations of production might change the elders into agents of the colonial bourgeoisie. Conflicts between the generations might then become the "locus" of certain class conflicts. However, this development must not be thought of as universal and necessary. It is more typical for class struggle to oppose not the old and the young, but either real agricultural entrepreneurs and wage laborers or sharecroppers, or small producers and processors, traders, transporters, etc. Moreover, in one way or another the administrative personnel appropriates a significant fraction of the surplus product of the peasant. In such circumstances I think that to overemphasize the antagonism between young and old would be a diversionary operation masking the real relations of exploitation which subordinate the peasant masses to the agricultural, commercial, and administrative bourgeoisie, which is itself in large measure an outpost of the bourgeoisie of the industrial-

Pierre-Philippe Rey and Georges Dupré did not consider the process of reproduction as a whole, but only at
the single moment of circulation; it may be this that led
them to see the relations between elder and junior as between exploiter and exploited. The errors into which this
attitude has led bourgeois political economy are common
knowledge. In the capitalist mode of production the
sphere of circulation is the foundation of the representation given to the sphere of production by the juridical and
ideological phases. The transformation of labor power
into a commodity and the existence of a circulation of
labor power bring about a maladjustment between the
structure of production and that of circulation: the first is
characterized by exploitation, the second by exchange. Society's awareness of its economic base rests on relations of
circulation and is inevitably deformed. Bourgeois economics reflects this consciousness and is, therefore, entangled
in a series of false problems: is the exchange between
worker and capitalist equal or unequal? Is labor sold at a
fair price? etc. . . . The bourgeois economist will answer
according to whether he is conservative or liberal. If, however, it is accepted that in every mode of production there
is a link between the "appearance" of circulation and the
image of production offered by the superstructure, then
we can ask if the existence within the mode of production
associated with simple cooperation of a circulation of
labor power, even though partial and non-mercantile, does
not produce a maladjustment analogous to what we no-
ticed in the capitalist mode of production. It is true that

---

ized country. In any case, these comments apply to socioeconomic formations already dominated by mercantile relations imposed by colonial
conquest and do not affect our conclusions about traditional socioeconomic formations drawn from the present attempt at analysis.

from the point of view of relations of production the circulation of wives appears as a distribution of labor power; but in the society's ideological concept of its economic base, this aspect pales before exchange relations, themselves simply the form taken by this distribution in the sphere of circulation. The ethnologist ratifies this "representation" when he isolates the moment of circulation in the process of reproduction: like the bourgeois economist he then asks himself whether the relations of circulation are the site of an equilibrium or an antagonism and his answer will depend upon whether he favors a static or a dynamic ethnology.

However, the various moments which make up the process of reproduction are not independent spheres governed by separate laws; they are determined by the relations of production. I have defined these as a distribution of the factors of production, a distribution which is both a condition and a consequence of the production process. Labor power is one of these factors and the circulation of wives "realizes" its distribution, and is also determined by the relations of production. These thus provide the point of departure for an analysis and explanation of the part played in this circulation by the elders. We have seen that the duality of the production community and the work-team implies the existence of the position of a controller of the distribution of the means of production; it seems to me probable that it also implies the existence of the position of a controller of the distribution of labor power. This occurs in two phases. The wives are first distributed between the production communities by the mechanism of generalized exchange; here the elder acts as the spokesman for his community in matrimonial negotiations but does not exercize any real power. Conflicts may erupt if one of the participant communities tries to discontinue the exchanges or divert them for its own benefit by abduction or refusal to pay its debts. Such conflicts, however, set one community against another and elders and juniors within each community would stand together in such a situation. So antagonism between elders and juniors does not apply to this first phase.

At the conclusion of the process the wife is acquired by the *production community* and, in a way, becomes its property: its members speak of her as "our wife"; if her husband were to die she would marry one of his brothers; etc. In the second phase, the production community requires that the available labor force be divided between its constituent work-teams: the wife might be allocated to a young bachelor, which would make possible the establishment of a new work-team, or to a married man, which would increase the personnel of the team he heads. It is this second phase of distribution which implies the existence of the position of controller; for, insofar as it takes the form of a circulation, it enters into the general system of tributes and redistributions which organize the process of circulation within the production community: means of production are entrusted to the juniors, who pay tribute in labor and in kind and, in return, receive both the means of subsistence and wives. Thus the distribution of the labor force, and that of the means of production and the product, compose a single process calling for one controller only. The elder plays the same part in matrimonial exchanges as he does in material production: in both cases his power is simply a function of his office.

The difference between the present analysis and that of Pierre-Philippe Rey and Georges Dupré is now apparent. To them the elder holds a monopoly on prestige-giving goods and thus controls the circulation of women and reinforces the dependence of the juniors: for me, the elder is first controller of the distribution of wives, and it is because he fulfils this role that prestige-goods are entrusted to him. To put it more generally, Rey and Dupré see the moment of tribute as determinant in the cycle of tributes and redistributions: the elder monopolizes the product of the labor of the juniors and hence presides over the redistribution. On the contrary, to me the moment of redistribution comes first and the moment of tribute is only its necessary consequence.

Finally, coming to method, Rey and Dupré regard the elders as a given social category, record their privileges, and deduce the existence of particular relations of production, in this case, relations of exploitation. My process is the reverse: for us the *persona* of the elder, and of the lineage system to which he belongs, result from production relations; these production relations must therefore be the starting point for determining his characteristics. Production relations determine the existence within the community of a function of controller of distribution, and the elder may be defined as *upholding* this function, subject to the *conditions* attached to its exercise. In the economic field these include the monopoly of prestige-giving goods and the concentration of the product in the hands of the elder; in the political and ideological field these include the authority of the elder—within the limits described earlier—his prestige, his social experience, etc. In other words, the elder's authority is super-determined by the different phases of the mode of production, and any analysis must distinguish between that aspect related to the structure of the production process and that related to the superstructural conditions in which it functions. The outcome of such an analysis may perhaps appear contrary to the appearances disclosed by ethnography but, as Marx said, scientific research would be useless if appearances and reality were identical.

CONCLUSION

This investigation is now complete. I do not hope to have adequately conveyed the richness of Claude Meillassoux's book; my purpose was more modest. Claude Meillassoux tried an experiment: taking Marxist concepts and analytical methods as working hypothoses, he sought to test their operational value in the field; it was my wish to emphasize the success of his experiment. *L'Anthropologie économique des Gouro* proves that the categories of historical materialism are perfectly applicable to so-called primitive societies, and that the study of such societies can be advanced by their use. In this sense Meillassoux is a pioneer: the discipline in which he works has up to now been entangled in various antagonistic ideologies—evolutionism, functionalism, culturalism, empirical or transcendental structuralism, etc.: he has opened the door to scientific knowledge.

One problem was raised at the beginning of this study and must be mentioned again, for it seems to me that the progress of any further research depends upon its solution: this is the concept of the mode of production which I understand quite differently from Meillassoux. It should be remembered that Meillassoux believes that the lineage-based and segmentary societies have a *single* mode of production, defined by the combination of a certain number of general economic features common to all such societies. I see a mode of production as a specific combination of a system of productive forces and a system of relations of production; bearing in mind the nature of the instruments of labor used in "primitive" socioeconomic formations, forms of cooperation are the keypoint at which the two systems are articulated. The number of different forms of cooperation found within any one such formation indicates the combined "presence" of as many distinct modes of production. This difference is both minor and major: minor within the limits of descriptive monographs, major for those who undertake comparative studies. In considering a single society there is no need to settle for one or the other definition: the first can be applied as well as the second, as long as the economic base of a single society is analyzed precisely enough, as was the case in *L'Anthropologie économique des Gouro*. On the other hand, if the purpose is to construct a general theory of pre-capitalist socioeconomic formations a choice becomes necessary. To repeat: if we assume that lineage-based and segmentary societies all have the *same* economic base operating the *same* mode of production—and that only the concrete conditions vary—we cannot hope to find in the economic infrastructure the explanation of the considerable differences which separate such societies at the level of social, juridical, political, and ideological superstructures. This amounts to an admission that historical materialism is not applicable to lineage-based and segmentary societies, leaving only an ideological "explanation." On the other hand, if we define the concept of a mode of production narrowly and precisely, each socioeconomic formation must appear as a complex combination of *several* modes of production. To quote from an unpublished manuscript by Louis Althusser, to whom I am indebted for this working hypothesis:

If one reads Marx, really listening to him, the following conclusions are unavoidable:

1. There are no primitive societies . . . there are social formations which we can provisionally call primitive, in a sense quite uncontaminated with ideas of origin.

2. Like any other social formation, the structure of a

primitive social formation can only be conceived through the concept of a mode of production with all the concepts subordinate to it, implied by it and contained within it (a mode of production actually comprises an economic base, a juridico-political superstructure, and an ideological super-structure).

3. Like any social formation, the structure of a primitive social formation is the result of the combination of at least two distinct modes of production, one of which is dominant and the other subordinate.

4. As in any other social formation, this combination of several modes of production (with one dominant over the other or others) produces specific effects which account for the concrete form taken on by the juridico-political and ideological superstructures.

The problem is how to construct a general description of so-called primitive socioeconomic formations within this framework. In the first place, the various modes of production realized in these formations must be listed, using as a guide a census of the forms of cooperation in use. This is what I have tried to do for the Guro. The next step should be to construct the theory of the modes of production identified; each socioeconomic formation would then appear to be composed of such and such modes of production combined in such fashion that one or other of them is dominant. Like a chemical molecule, a socioeconomic formation would then be defined by its composition as well as its structure, by the nature of its component elements as well as by the way they are organized within the whole. The interplay of these variables would make it possible to account for the diversity of the juridical, political, and ideological superstructures discovered by the ethnographer.

It may be that Meillassoux limited himself to the idea

that the whole of any lineage-based or segmentary society rests upon a single mode of production because he has not quite given up the ideological conviction that the so-called primitive societies have an irreducible specificity derived, in the final analysis, from their simplicity, homogeneity, and limpidity. We must be clear about these terms: classical social anthropology certainly perceived the variety and complexity of the societies and cultures which were its subject of study; it quite legitimately tried to reduce, or at any rate to bring order into, this variety and complexity. But to this end cultures and societies were considered "expressive totalities," a term which Althusser defines as

> a totality all of whose parts are so many "*total parts*," each expressing the others, and each expressing the social totality that contains them, because each in itself contains in the immediate form of its expression the essence of the totality itself. . . .
>
> The Leibnizian concept of expression . . . presupposes in principle that the whole in question be reducible to an *inner essence*, of which the elements of the whole are then no more than the phenomenal forms of expression, the inner principle of the essence being present at each point in the whole, such that at each moment it is possible to write the immediately adequate equation: *such and such an element* (economic, political, legal, literary, religious, etc., in Hegel) = *the inner essence of the whole*.[32]

Classical social anthropology offers several definitions of this "inner essence of the whole," of this principle that allows the integration of the social totality. It may be biological in nature; this leads to the functionalism of Malinowski, in which this unifying role is attributed to organic needs:

> Every culture must satisfy the biological system of needs, such as those dictated by metabolism, reproduction, the

physiological conditions of temperature, protection from moisture, wind, and the direct impact of damaging forces of climate and weather, safety from dangerous animals or human beings, occasional relaxation, the exercise of the muscular nervous system in movement, and the regulation of growth. . . . *Every cultural achievement* that implies the use of artifacts and symbolism is an *instrumental enhancement of human anatomy, and refers directly or indirectly to the satisfaction of a bodily need.*[33]

A definition of the "inner essence of the whole" can equally be sought in psychology: this leads to the theory of "basic personality," or to the theories of Ruth Benedict and Margaret Mead. The latter expresses it as follows:

This hypothesis is an extension of that advanced by Ruth Benedict in her *Patterns of Culture.* Let us assume that there are definite temperamental differences between human beings which if not entirely hereditary at least are established on a hereditary base very soon after birth. (Further than this we cannot at present narrow the matter.) These differences finally embodied in the character structure of adults, then, are the clues from which culture works, selecting one temperament, or a combination of related and congruent types, as desirable, and *embodying this choice in every thread of the social fabric*—in the care of the young child, the games the children play, the songs the people sing, the structure of political organization, the religious observance, the art and the philosophy.[34]

It is also possible to find the "inner essence of the whole" in a purely formal principle, and it then appears that the integration of the social totality occurs not on the semantic level, but on the level of syntax. This can be seen in the structuralism of Claude Lévi-Strauss. Sometimes he seeks homologies among the various levels of social reality —language, kinship, myth. In a study of the relations between myth and kinship among the Pueblo Indians, he writes that myth

> is no longer a progressive linear movement, it is a system of polar oppositions, such as we find in the kinship system. Now if it is true that these features of the *kinship system can be correlated with systems belonging to a completely different field, the field of mythology,* we are entitled to ask the linguist whether or not something of the same kind does not show up in the field of language. *And it would be very surprising if something*—I do not know exactly what, because I am not a linguist—*could not be found to exist,* because if the answer should be in the negative, we should have to assume that, while fields that are so wide apart as kinship and mythology nevertheless succeed in remaining correlated, language and mythology, which are much more closely related, show no connection or no communication whatsoever.[35]

Lucien Sebag states it more categorically:

> Logic has primacy in relation to the different levels of social organization which appear as *so many different realizations of this logic* corresponding to man's various purposes.[36]

Sometimes Lévi-Strauss adopts a more subtle approach, assuming that the relations between these levels of social reality can vary greatly. However, for any given society he maintains that the transformations which occur in passing from one level to another belong to the same family: this is the idea of an "order of orders":

> By *order of orders*, then, I mean the formal properties of the whole made up of subwholes, each of which corresponds to a given structural level. . . .
>
> I do not postulate a kind of pre-existent harmony between the different levels of structure. They may be—and often are—completely contradictory, but the modes of contradiction *all belong to the same type.* . . .

If we grant, following Marxian thought, that infrastructures and superstructures are made up of multiple levels and that there are various types of transformation from one level to another, it becomes possible—in the final analysis, and on the condition that we disregard content—to *characterize different types of societies in terms of the types of transformations* which occur within them. These types of transformations amount to formulas showing the number, magnitude, direction, and order of the convolutions that must be unraveled, so to speak, in order to uncover (logically, not normatively) an ideal homologous relationship between the different structural levels.[37]

Finally, the structuralism of A. R. Radcliffe-Brown can be described as empirical precisely because it affirms the integration of the whole without establishing the principal on which this integration takes place. The "reciprocal expression" of the various parts of the totality is here presented as truly axiomatic.

In historical materialism this reciprocal expression is replaced by a reciprocal determination between elements whose originality as such is irreducible. Marxism is fundamentally alien to all theories of reflection or generation: the elements of the whole neither reflect each other nor generate each other; they are always given in advance within a "structure articulated by a dominant," a structure which determines the nature and limits of the effects which they may have upon each other.

Marx established all this for social formations dominated by the capitalist mode of production. The ideology of "expressive totality" then ebbed into the field of social anthropology and soon served to define the very subject matter of this discipline. "Reciprocal expression" between the elements within a whole was presented as a specific characteristic of the societies studied by the social anthropologists, as a special difference separating them from industrialized societies, which were to be left to historical materialism. It was hoped that this would ensure the autonomy of social anthropology. Marxist researchers now face the task of ferreting this ideology out of its last refuge, of bringing the field so far reserved for social anthropology within the ambit of historical materialism, and thus demonstrating the universal validity of the concepts and methods developed by the latter. By doing this they should ensure that social anthropology becomes a particular section of historical materialism devoted to socioeconomic formations in which the capitalist mode of production is absent and in which ethnologists and historians collaborate. It is to Claude Meillassoux's great credit that he initiated this task and took the first steps on a long and difficult road.

Notes

1. All references in parentheses refer to Claude Meillassoux, *L'Anthropologie économique des Gouro de Côte d'Ivoire* (Paris, 1964).—*Trans.*
2. Etienne Balibar, "On the Basic Concepts of Historical Materialism," Chapter 2, in Louis Althusser and Etienne Balibar, *Reading Capital* (New York: Pantheon Books, 1970).
3. Karl Marx, *Capital* (London: Progress Publishers, 1970), vol. 1, p. 330–331.
4. Ibid., p. 180.
5. Balibar, "The Basic Concepts of Historical Materialism," pp. 239 ff.
6. André Leroi-Gourhan, *Le Geste et la parole* (Paris: Editions Albin Michel, 1965), vol. 2, pp. 41 and 47.
7. Marx, *Capital*, vol. 1, p. 373.
8. On this, see Emmanuel Terray, "L'Organisation sociale des Dida, essai sur un village Dida de la région de Lakota," mimeographed

(Abidjan, Ivory Coast: University of Abidjan, Ethno-Sociological Institute), pp. 82 ff.

9. Marx, *Capital*, vol. 1, p. 326.

10. Ibid., p. 180.

11. Karl Marx, *Grundrisse der Kritik der Politischen Ökonomie* (Berlin: Dietz Verlag, 1953), p. 378.

12. Louis Tauxier, *Nègres Gouro et Gagou* (Paris: Guethner, 1924); Ariane Deluz, "Villages et lignages chez les Gouro de Côte d'Ivoire," *Cahiers d'Etudes Africaines*, vol. 1, no. 19, pp. 388–452.

13. Claude Meillassoux, "Recherche d'un niveau de détermination dans la société cynégétique," *L'Homme et la Société*, no. 6 (October–December 1967), p. 100.

14. Claude Meillassoux, "Essai d'interprétation de phénomène economique dans les sociétés traditionnelles d'auto-subsistance," *Cahiers d'Etudes Africaines*, no. 4 (December 1960).

15. Ibid., p. 47.

16. Ibid.

17. On this see Karl Polanyi, "The Economy as Instituted Process," in Karl Polanyi, Conrad Arensberg, Harry W. Pearson, eds., *Trade and Market in the Early Empires* (Glencoe, Ill.: The Free Press, 1957), p. 250.

18. Letter from Engels to Marx, December 8, 1882, in *Correspondence of Karl Marx and Friedrich Engels* (New York: International Publishers, 1934), p. 405.

19. Claude Lévi-Strauss, interview in *Témoignage chrétien*, April 8, 1968, p. 18.

20. Meillassoux, "Recherche d'un niveau de détermination," p. 98.

21. Maurice Godelier, *Rationaliste et irrationaliste en économie* (Paris: François Maspero éditeur, 1968), p. 91.

22. From a personal communication to the author.

23. From a personal communication to the author.

24. See Terray, "L'Organisation sociale des Dida."

25. Marx, *Grundrisse*, p. 137.

26. Ibid., p. 134.

27. Pierre-Philippe Rey, "Le Mode de production lignager," unpublished manuscript.

28. Karl Marx, *A Contribution to the Critique of Political Economy* (Chicago: Charles H. Kerr & Company, 1904), pp. 302–3.

29. Georges Dupré, Pierre-Philippe Rey, "Théorie de l'histoire des échanges, exemple de l'Ouest Congolais (Congo-Brazzaville)," unpublished manuscript, p. 30.

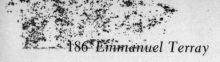
30. Ibid., p. 33.
31. Ariane Deluz and Maurice Godelier, "Apropos de deux textes d'anthropologie économique," *L'Homme*, vol. 8, no. 3 (1967), p. 86.
32. Louis Althusser, "The Object of *Capital*," in Althusser & Balibar, *Reading Capital*, pp. 40 and 167.
33. Bronislaw Malinowski, *A Scientific Theory of Culture and Other Essays* (Chapel Hill: University of North Carolina Press, 1944), p. 171. My italics.—E.T.
34. Margaret Mead, *Sex and Temperament in Three Primitive Societies* (New York: Dell Publishing, 1963), p. 263.
35. Claude Lévi-Strauss, *Structural Anthropology* (Garden City, N.Y.: Doubleday & Company, Inc., An Anchor Book, 1967), p. 75.
36. Lucien Sebag, *Marxisme et structuralisme* (Paris: Editions Payot, 1964), p. 149. My italics.—E.T.
37. Lévi-Strauss, *Structural Anthropology*, pp. 329–30. My italics.—E.T.